THE DELINQUENT GIRL

THE

DELINQUENT

GIRL

By

CLYDE B. VEDDER, Ph.D.

Department of Sociology and Anthropology
Illinois State University
Normal, Illinois

and

DORA B. SOMERVILLE, ACSW

Correctional Program Executive
Illinois Department of Corrections
Springfield, Illinois

With a Foreword by
ALLYN R. SIELAFF

Director, Department of Corrections
State of Illinois

HV
6046
.V4
1975

181102

CHARLES C THOMAS · PUBLISHER
Springfield · Illinois · U. S. A.

Published and Distributed Throughout the World by
CHARLES C THOMAS · PUBLISHER
BANNERSTONE HOUSE
301-327 East Lawrence Avenue, Springfield, Illinois, U.S.A.

© *1973 and 1975 by* CHARLES C THOMAS · PUBLISHER
ISBN 0-398-03260-2

Library of Congress Catalog Card Number 74-9669

Library of Congress Cataloging in Publication Data
Vedder, Clyde Bennett, 1903–
   The delinquent girl.

   1. Delinquent girls—United States. I. Somerville, Dora B., joint author.
II. Title. [DNLM: 1. Juvenile delinquency. HV9069 V415d]
HV6046.V4 1974   364.36'4'0973   74-9669
ISBN 0-398-03260-2

Printed in the United States of America
HH-11

FOREWORD

Juvenile Delinquency is not a new phenomenon; boys and girls have been "getting into trouble" for a long time. According to Charles Dickens, Oliver Twist was a notorious delinquent. Twenty years ago juvenile gangs were romanticized by the Sharks and Jets in *West Side Story*.

For far too long, most people have had a remote and distorted view of juvenile delinquency. However, more recently the public has had access to more realistic information. Our public policies have begun to reflect a more humane and rational approach to the problem of children in trouble. During the past decade, much more serious attention has been given to the causes, prevention and control of delinquency; to the personality characteristics of delinquents in confinement; to rehabilitation programs; and, to juvenile diversionary programs from the criminal justice system.

In this book, Miss Dora B. Somerville and Dr. Clyde Vedder present new insights into the special problems of delinquent girls—an historically neglected subject. They offer a text, written for both laymen and professionals in law enforcement and corrections, which contains theoretical concepts of delinquency and crime as well as significant case histories.

Dr. Vedder, Professor of Sociology at Illinois State University, Normal, Illinois, has written extensively on the subject of juvenile delinquency. He has had regular contact with delinquent boys and girls and with the professional staff who counsel them through his long and valued association with the former Illinois Youth Commission, and now as a member of the Advisory Board to the Illinois Department of Corrections—Juvenile Division. Miss Somerville holds a Master's Degree in Social Work with a psychiatric sequence from Loyola University of Chicago, and a Master's Degree in Child Study from the School of Social Sciences, Catholic University of America, Washington, D. C. She is a former member of Illinois' first full time, professional Parole and Pardon Board, the first woman to be appointed. Prior to this

v

appointment in 1969, she was for eight years, a member of the Illinois Youth Commission.

Other important positions held by Miss Somerville include Director of the Social Service Department, Psychiatric Institute, Circuit Court of Cook County, and Program Coordinator at the Illinois State Training School for Girls, Geneva, Illinois. Her current position is that of Correctional Program Executive of the Illinois Department of Corrections where among her many responsibilities, she is coordinator of the internship and student field placement program for the Department.

The authors, for whom I have a great deal of respect, both personally and professionally, are to be commended for their outstanding work. This effort is a most useful contribution in a field where there are no readily available easy answers.

Allyn R. Sielaff

PREFACE

Few social problems arouse deeper concern throughout the world than those associated with juvenile delinquency and crime. Besides the natural affection which adults have for children, especially frustrated and neglected children, the knowledge that a happy and wholesome child is the best guarantee for a stable society impels lavish expenditures of time, energy and money toward solving the problem of juvenile delinquency and crime. However, even though society attempts to arrest or to eradicate the development of a social or antisocial tendencies, delinquent behavior still exists.

The limitations and alleged failures of corrections is being given much attention recently, especially by the experts in the field of criminal justice. Mass incarceration, particularly in remote areas is receiving in-depth re-evaluation. Community based treatment and diversionary programs are popular subjects today and have been implemented with positive results in several states.

There have been references to delinquency from the earliest times. Three hundred years ago, John Locke, the great English philosopher, deplored delinquency in the same manner as we do today. Six thousand years ago, an Egyptian priest carved in a rock: "Our earth degenerate. . . . Children no longer obey their parents." Yet the term "juvenile delinquency" is not as old as the phenomenon we recognize and know. Children with behavior problems, who today are labeled "delinquent," were formerly referred to as "depraved," "headstrong," "wayward," or simply "waifs and strays." It is believed that the term "delinquent" was used first in 1823 when a group of New York educators and philanthropists formed a society for the prevention of juvenile delinquency and opened an institution known as the "House of Refuge."

No one familiar with the subject of juvenile delinquency would minimize its seriousness. The concern felt for "problem children" is shared not only by law enforcement officials and juvenile court judges and criminal justice officials but also by social workers, sociologists, chaplains, psychologists and psychiatrists. This concern is shared by civic and social clubs, school officials and interested and informed parents. Consequently, many persons engaged in the behavioral and social sciences and in criminal justice programs have advanced various theories and approaches in dealing with this perplexing problem.

Juvenile delinquency means different things to different people. It stems from a myriad of interacting forces and has many overt forms. To some, a juvenile delinquent is a boy or girl arrested for a law violation. To many, the term covers a variety of antisocial behavior which offends them, whether or not a law is violated. Legally, the term "juvenile delinquent" applies to a boy or girl adjudged delinquent by a juvenile court. Yet, offenders who become involved with the police and courts represent only a segment of juvenile law violators. Some who engage in delinquent behavior are not apprehended.

The causes of juvenile delinquency are multiple. All factors—physical, mental, emotional, and social—must be considered to determine the causative factors. An effective course of treatment should be instituted in order to deal with and to focus on attacking the causes rather than to concentrate exclusively on the symptoms. All factors contributing to the causes of delinquency and crime should be vigorously attacked.

State laws differ as to the maximum age which determines whether a young offender will be handled as a juvenile delinquent or an adult criminal. Eighteen is the upper limit in most states; in other states it is sixteen or seventeen. Some state laws require that persons of juvenile age be tried in an adult criminal court for certain crimes, e.g. murder. In many states the juvenile court can waive jurisdiction so that a juvenile is tried in an adult criminal court for felonious offenses.

In the State of Illinois, the Unified Code of Corrections raises the age at which a minor may be confined in a jail from 14 to 16 years of age. It limits commitment to the Department of Corrections to those delinquent minors who have committed an offense which could be punished by incarceration if committed by an adult. The Code generally provides for commitment to the Department of Corrections of juveniles under 13 years of age.[1]

Juvenile delinquents display several of these characteristics: a lack of self-confidence and self-esteem; a lack of a feeling of being likeable and worthwhile individuals; a lack of parental love and affection; a search for excitement—wild, daring things to do; a dissatisfaction with school; and a rebellious and resistive attitude toward authority.

Statistical and sociological studies show that the proportion of women to men has been steadily increasing in the population, in the labor market, in the control of wealth and in the commission of crime. In 1966 the Chicago Police Department reported that in addition to the increase of runaways from home, girls were also becoming involved in more aggressive types of crime at a faster rate than boys.[2]

The Federal Bureau of Investigation reported that although male arrests for all crimes outnumbered female arrests, female arrests continue to increase more rapidly, especially those under the age of eighteen. From 1960 to 1970, male arrests increased 25.7 per cent, female arrests 74.4 per cent. Male arrests under eighteen years of age increased by 204.1 per cent.[3]

Because of a paucity of published material on both the delinquent girl and the factors which contribute to her increasing delinquency, the authors felt that these phenomena should be explored further. The authors sent a questionnaire to all state institutions for delinquent girls to ascertain the offenses leading to institutional commitment. Comparisons were made between other states and the state of Illinois on the frequency of offenses. In the section following the analysis of principle offenses which lead to commitment, case histories of the girls involved in these offenses are given as well as the story of the delinquent girl as told in her own words. This also includes an analysis of some of the dynamics which led to her delinquency. This study, the case histories, the

---

1 "Summary-Illinois Unified Code of Corrections" Printed by authority of the State of Illinois, August, 1972.

2 Frances Herb, "What is Our Miss-Behavior?" Paper presented at the 36th Annual Governor's Conference on Youth, Sherman House, Chicago, Illinois, April 4, 1966.

3 Federal Bureau of Investigation, *Uniform Crime Reports*, 1970, p. 124.

girls' own accounts of their situations and subsequent commitment, will hopefully furnish criminal justice workers, the practi-
tioner in juvenile probation, parole and law enforcement, the correctional worker, the teacher and student and all involved in the
control, treatment and prevention of juvenile delinquency with
greater insights into the field of female delinquency.

While studying delinquent girls let us keep this thought in
mind: When you train a man, you train an individual; when you
train a woman, you train a family. The girls are speaking to all
of us:

> We are the young; our tender years are turning tough. Whether
> we sit before classroom books or waste our time on neighbor-
> hood blocks, we face a future of computers, conveyors and con-
> fusion. The challenges to us are countless and sometimes in-
> surmountable. While many of us will rise to these challenges,
> some of us cannot by ourselves. Help us to find our way. . . .
> please![4]

[4] Doris T. Snell

PROLOGUE TO THE SECOND EDITION

The favorable acceptance of the First Edition of *The Delinquent Girl* and other trends related to the increase rate and character of female delinquency and to the decreased rate of commitment to Illinois' correctional institutions justify the updating of certain statistical data and substantiates the revelancy for a second edition of this book.

In the middle 1960's the most frequent offenses leading to the commitment of girls to the Illinois State Training School for Girls was runaway. In order of frequency runaway was followed by incorrigibility, sex delinquency, probation violation, and truancy. For the period July 1972 through June 1973, the Illinois State Training School for Girls report runaway also to be the leading reason for commitment. However, in order of frequency, for this period runaway was followed by theft; battery; burglary, probation violation, strong armed robbery; violation of court order and narcotics.

The following comparative data selected from the types of petitions filed in Circuit Court of Cook County—Juvenile Division, for females for the years 1971 and 1972 respectively provide interesting and significant material for this revised edition:

Delinquent Petitions and Counts	1971	—	1972
Assault	607	—	616
Other Delinquent Behavior	465	—	411
Theft	313	—	307
Violation of Court Order	241	—	112
Narcotics	116	—	134
Burglary	116	—	95
Robbery	113	—	84
Criminal Damage to Property	92	—	57
Automobile Theft and Trespass	90	—	81
Unlawful Use of Weapons	75	—	64
Homicide	12	—	10

Arson .... 11 — 6
Glue Sniffing .... 9 — 7

Supervision Petitions   1971 — 1972
Runaway ....1960 — 1428
Truancy (Habitual) .... 59 — 12
Ungovernable .... 541 — 353
Other Supervision Petitions .... 124 — 64

This data illustrates the dramatic change in the character of the offenses of female juvenile delinquents. Assault, burglary, and strong armed robbery in the past were considered characteristic of male offenses. Other offenses also appearing in official records, such as arson, automobile theft, robbery, criminal damage to property; unlawful use of weapon and homicide will be revealed in various data supplied by the 1972 Uniform Crime Reports, Federal Bureau of Investigation and from other governmental and private agencies.

We shall implement the girl's own stories by the inclusion of the new categories of female juvenile offenses which lead to their commitment to the Illinois Department of Corrections, Juvenile Division.

ACKNOWLEDGMENTS

The unfailing cooperation of the superintendents of the various training schools for delinquent girls is deeply appreciated. They contributed greatly to the compiling of data in order to make this book relevant to current practices. Dr. Russell H. Levy, Director of Research and Long Range Planning, Illinois Department of Corrections, was most helpful in making available and interpreting relevant statistical data on the female juvenile offender.

We are especially indebted to Miss Frances Nickmann, former Superintendent of the Illinois State Training School for Girls; Geneva, Illinois, former Assistant Superintendent, Mr. Robert J. Harrington and staff members Mr. Thomas Oki and Miss Rena Dean who assisted Mr. Stanley Levine, present Assistant Superintendent, in the selection and in the analysis of case material. For the girls' own stories, whose names remain anonymous, we are most grateful to them for relating accounts of their own stories which contributed greatly to the human interest element in this book; and, which graphically relates some theoretical concepts to reality situations.

We are indeed grateful also to coauthor Dora Somerville's brother, Dr. Addison Somerville, and his wife, Carolyn, and Mrs. Joan Massaquoi for their assistance in the analysis of the individual stories of the girls. To Miss Somerville's niece, Ann, and her husband, Dr. Charles Jones, the authors are greatly appreciative for their invaluable help. We are especially indebted to Mr. Anthony Sorrentino, Superintendent, Community Services (Cook County) Juvenile Division, Illinois Department of Corrections; to Mrs. Elizabeth Ciancone; to Miss Betty Begg, Director, Division of Corrections, Department of Human Resources, City of Chicago, Eileen B. Vedder, wife of senior author, and especially, to Rev. Christopher Janowski, O.F.M., who gave generously of their time to edit, to criticize, and to suggest certain changes in the drafts of this book. The editorial assistance of all of these individuals and that of Joan and Hans Massaquoi is very much appreciated.

The provocative discussions with Mr. John P. Dohm, member of the Illinois Parole and Pardon Board, resulted in the exploration of several areas of female delinquency, not originally considered in the earlier drafting of this book.

Our sincere gratitude to Captain Michael Delaney, former Director, Youth Division, Chicago Police Department, and to James B. Conlisk, Jr., Superintendent, and to Mrs. Frances Herb of the Youth Division of the Chicago Police Department for their help in collecting statistics pertaining to juvenile delinquency and crime in the Chicago area and Joseph Puntil, Project Director, Institute for Juvenile Research. Mr. John O'Brien, former Director of Clinical Services, Juvenile Court of Cook County and Mr. Seymour J. Adler, Director of Court Services, Circuit Court of Cook County, Illinois County Department, Juvenile Division, were also very helpful in providing pertinent statistical material.

We are especially grateful to Miss Somerville's niece, Doris T. Snell, for providing a frame of reference for this book with her unique contributions of the poem and for her artistic ability in designing the book's jacket, and to Eileen McLeod Vedder for her painstaking effort in reading every word of the manuscript and making several worthwhile suggestions.

In completing the first edition, Mrs. Sarah Smith was very helpful in arranging for secretarial assistance. Mrs. Dorene Moore, Mrs. Ella Miller, Mrs. Charlotte Halls, Mrs. Patricia Brazil, Mrs. Kathlyn Burkee, and Mrs. Caroline Grant contributed generously of their leisure time in laboriously typing various sections of the drafts of this book. For the second edition, Miss Lillian Calhoun and Mrs. Caroline Grant also assisted in the typing of the manuscript.

The patience, understanding and encouragement of our families and friends were indispensible in our study of this long and neglected subject.

We are indebted to all who contributed to the completion of both editions of this book and we dedicate it to our families, our friends, and to all those committed persons concerned about the welfare of the delinquent girl.

C.B.V.
D.B.S.

CONTENTS

THE DELINQUENT GIRL

CHAPTER **I**

INTRODUCTION

THE MOST FREQUENT OFFENSES leading to the commitment of girls to the Illinois Department of Corrections—Juvenile Division are well known to practitioners in the field of Juvenile deliquency in the State of Illinois. But what about the other forty-nine States? As reported in the first edition of *The Delinquent Girl,* a questionnaire was sent to the proper authorities of all public training schools in other states for female juvenile delinquents listed in the *Directory of Public Training Schools,* published by the U. S. Department of Health, Education and Welfare. Out of eighty-five inquiries, approximately 70 per cent responded, including some follow-up inquiries. The responses represented the major geographic regions of the United States, except Alaska and Hawaii, and reflected the calendar year of 1963.

Returns from the questionnaire provided significant information. There was considerable variation in the average length of stay, from six months to twenty months. The average stay in all states was about ten and one-half months. Other variations observed in institutional populations of girls' training schools ranged from thirty-one to more than five hundred girls.

The California Youth Authority reports[1] that from the period between 1965 and 1972 the general trend has been toward longer periods of confinements which includes time spent in the clinics for diagnosis. The length of stay for all wards in all types of institutions rose from 9.4 months in 1965 to 11.1 months in 1972. For males, the length of stay increased from 9.6 months in 1965 to 11.2 months in 1972: for females from 7.9 months to 10.3 months. It reports further that institutional length of stay is affected by

3

such factors as changes in Youth Authority Board policy, changes in characteristic of wards, institutional population pressures, and changing emphasis in programming.

The incidents of black girls in racially nonsegregated institutional populations ranged from 1 per cent to 70 per cent. In some geographical areas, the small percentage reflected the small percentages of blacks in the general population. In the large metropolitan areas, delinquent girls accounted for approximately 50 to 70 per cent of the institutional female population. Similar to the concentration of girls in some state training schools, in the states having concentrations of national-group population, delinquent girls of Mexican, Indian, or Puerto Rican extraction were committed in ratios of three to four times higher than their rate in the general population.

The questionnaire returns also revealed that the states' costs for the maintenance of institutionalized girls varied dramatically—ranging from $1,100 to $6,680 per girl. However, most institutions reported a cost of between $2,000 and $3,300 per girl in the early 1960's. Today, costs vary $5,000 to $15,000 per annum. There is no dearth of *reasons* leading to commitment or return to a state training school. Fairly representative of the charges which can lead to commitment are the following: operating a car unlawfully, disorderly conduct, aggravated battery, resisting arrest, defying parental authority, setting fires, passing bogus checks, voluntary manslaughter, probation violation, running away, incorrigibility, sex delinquency, poor adjustment, curfew violation, assault, truancy, shoplifting, forgery, auto theft, pregnancy, drinking, burglary, soliciting-prostitution and fighting.

In Illinois, the major offenses leading to commitment to the former Illinois Youth Commission, in order of frequency, were as follows: runaway, incorrigibility, sex delinquency, probation violation and truancy. The order is subject to slight variation from time to time. With the exception of "poor adjustment," which could include more than one of the above offenses, the categories referred to above are classified as the "big five" reasons leading to the commitment of delinquent girls in Illinois. It was anticipated that returns from the questionnaire would show other states reporting the same reasons leading to commitment, possibly even in the same order. And in fact, regardless of geographic location, most training schools for girls reported a distribution of offenses similar to the "big five," with runaway occupying first place, incorrigibility second place and sex delinquency usually third. Beyond third place there was considerable variations in the reasons for commitment.

A great variety of offenses fall under the various states' definitions of juvenile delinquency. Sussman[2] lists such offenses in the order of frequency in which they occur in the various state statutes:

1. Violation of a law or ordinance.
2. Habitual truancy.
3. Association with known thieves, vicious or immoral persons.
4. Incorrigibility.
5. Being beyond control of parent or guardian.
6. Growing up in idleness or crime.
7. Deporting self so as to injure or endanger self or others.
8. Absence from home without parent's or guardian's consent.
9. Immoral or indecent conduct.
10. Habitual use of vile, obscene or vulgar language.
11. Visits to a known house of ill repute.
12. Patronizing or visiting policy shop or gaming place.
13. Habitual wandering about railroad yards or tracks.
14. Jumping train or entering car or engine without authority.
15. Patronizing saloon or dram shop where intoxicating liquor is sold.
16. Wandering streets at night while not on lawful business.
17. Patronizing public poolroom or bucket shop.
18. Immoral conduct around school.
19. Engaging in an illegal occupation.
20. Engaging in occupation or situation dangerous or injurious to one's self or others.
21. Smoking cigarettes or using tobacco in any form.
22. Frequenting a place whose existence violates law.
23. Being found in a place permitting activities for which an adult may be punished.

24. Addiction to drugs.
25. Disorderly conduct.
26. Begging.
27. Use of intoxicating liquor.
28. Making indecent proposals.
29. Loitering, sleeping in alleys, vagrancy.
30. Running away from state or charity institutions.
31. Being found on premises occupied or used for illegal purposes.
32. Operating a motor vehicle dangerously or while under influence of liquor.
33. Attempting to marry without consent, in violation of law.
34. Sexual irregularities.

A significant change in the "big five" offenses is indicated from the data based on data secured from the 1970 Annual Report.[3] In Illinois, in 1970 the major offenses leading to commitment of girls to the Illinois Department of Corrections, Juvenile Division, in order of frequency, were as follows: 1) Violation of Probation, 2) Larceny, 3) Assault, 4) Burglary, and 5) Carrying Concealed Weapon. In the 1970 Annual Report of the California Youth Authority, the number of commitments for narcotic and drug offenses more than doubled between 1965 and 1970. For California girls the most common offenses were incorrigibility, runaway, and foster home failure, followed closely by narcotic and drug offenses. Eighty seven percent had three or more delinquent contacts prior to commitment to the Youth Authority. Sixty two per cent had used marijuana or dangerous drugs while 22 per cent had used opiates.

The 1972 Annual Report of the California Youth Authority[4] reports that the total number of offenses or reasons for commitment of females first commitments placed under Youth Authority custody was 252. For males, the total number was 2,476. In order of frequency or highest number the reasons were incorrigible and runaway (50), narcotics and drugs (39), foster home failure (35), assault and battery (24), and, escape from county facilities (21). California further reports that the male/female components of the Youth Authority commitments are showing a trend toward a larger proportions of males. In 1965, approximately 84 per cent of all commitments were males. By 1972 this had increased to 91 per cent and it is anticipated that this trend will continue.

The following profile of a California Youth Authority male and female juvenile first commitment as reported in 1972 Annual Report provide a significant summary:

A California Youth Authority Male

His Home Environment
1. Fifty-four per cent came from a below average socioeconomic environment, with 37 per cent from an environment judged to be average and 9 per cent above average.
2. A significant number (36%) came from homes where all or part of the family income was from public assistance, but the majority (64%) came from homes which were economically self-supporting.

His Family
1. Sixty-two per cent had parents who were not living together at the time of commitment either because of divorce or separation (47%) or death (15%).
2. Forty-one per cent had one or both parents who had completed high school. For 23 per cent, neither parent had gone beyond the eighth grade.

His Schooling
1. Attitude toward school was judged to be indifferent or negative for 70 per cent of the males, with the remaining 30 per cent having a positive attitude.
2. Fifty-seven per cent had been involved in serious school misbehavior on more than an occasional basis. Only 13 per cent had no record of serious school misbehavior.

His Delinquent Behavior
1. Eighty-seven per cent had three or more delinquent contacts prior to commitment to the Youth Authority and 44 per cent had nine or more.
2. Eighty-three per cent had friends who tended towards a delinquent orientation.

A California Youth Authority Female

Her Home Environment
1. Fifty-four per cent came from a below average age socioeconomic environment with 40 per cent from an environment judged to be average and 6 per cent above average.
2. A significant number (34%) came from homes where all or part of the family income was from public assistance, but the majority (66%) came from homes which were economically self-supporting.

Her Family
1. Sixty-nine per cent had parents who were not living together at the time of commitment either due to divorce or separation (55%) or death (14%).
2. Forty-six per cent had one or more parents who had completed high school. For 21 per cent, neither parent had gone beyond the eighth grade.

Her Schooling
1. Attitude towards school was judged to be positive for only 24 per cent of the wards while for the remaining 76 per cent it was judged to be indifferent or negative.
2. Sixty-six per cent had been involved in serious school misbehavior on more than an occasional basis. Only 11 per cent had no record of serious school misbehavior.

Her Delinquent Behavior
1. Eighty-five per cent had three or more delinquent contacts prior to commitment to the Youth Authority and 32 per cent had nine or more.
2. Eighty-seven per cent had friends who tended towards a delinquent orientation.

From the legal standpoint, juvenile delinquency combines characteristics of social protection and restriction. This is evident in Sussman's list, having the purpose of protecting minors as it limits their rights and makes illegal certain activities only permitted for adults, e. g 5, 15, 17. While these offenses appear most often in the statutes, only two violations appear in the "big five":

incorrigibility and truancy. Most offenses would be included automatically as listed by Sussman—violation of any law or ordinance.

Male and female adolescents begin delinquent acts in early childhood. Police apprehended them as young as six to seven years of age. Girls below the age of twelve are guilty primarily of shoplifting, the same offense of which preadolscent boys are guilty. Numerous studies of juvenile delinquency, e.g. the Gluecks, are limited to males; studies of delinquent females are scarce. Female offenses tend to harm girls, but this harm is outgrown as girls' mature. Minor sex offenses, e.g. promiscuity, are often curbed by marriage. Female delinquency can be more serious than male delinquency, for if girls carry their problems into marriage, their lack of adjustment may affect the child-rearing of either sons or daughters. Perhaps one way to curb male delinquency is to give more attention to female delinquency.

In the 1972 edition of Uniform Crime Reports,[5] the Federal Bureau of Investigation reported that arrests of juveniles under 18 years of age, for all types of offenses combined, more than doubled ($+125\%$ between 1960 and 1972). For a group of serious offenses such as criminal homicide, forcible rape, burglary, robbery, aggravated assault, larceny and auto theft, the combined increase was 107 per cent between 1960 and 1972. The five-year arrest trends, 1967 to 1972, revealed that arrests for young females under 18 increased 62 per cent, while arrests for young males under 18 rose 21 per cent. When serious crimes as a group were considered, arrest of males in 1967 to 1972 were up 18 per cent and female arrests up 72 per cent.[6] According to police arrest data, all types of offenses—serious as well as relatively minor— have increased with the most serious one showing substantially greater proportionate increase. However, serious offenses against persons represent only 3 per cent of all arrests of juveniles.

Although the delinquency rate is higher for boys, the disparity between the number of boys' and girls' delinquency court cases is decreasing.

From 1970 to 1972, nationally, girls cases referred to courts increased almost twice as much as the boys' cases. There was an 11 per cent increase for girls' cases as compared to a 6 per cent increase for boys' cases with the larger increase in girls' cases occurring in urban, semi-urban and in rural courts.

The U. S. Department of Health, Education, and Welfare reports that in 1971 girls' delinquency cases disposed of by juvenile courts have been rising faster than those of boys every year since 1965. Between 1965 and 1971, girls delinquency cases increased by 97 per cent whereas boys cases increased by 52 per cent. ✓

The U. S. Department of Health, Education and Welfare reports that over one million (1,125,000) juvenile delinquency cases, excluding traffic offenses were estimated as being handled by all juvenile courts in the United States in 1971. The estimated number of children involved in these cases (970,000) was lower however, since in some instances, the same child was referred more than once during the year. These children represent 2.9 per cent of all children aged 10 to 18 in the country.

It is reported further that in 1971 more than half (58%) of the delinquency cases disposed of by juvenile courts were handled nonjudicially, that is without the filing of a petition. Because of the availability of probation staff in the larger courts, the proportion of cases handled nonjudicially was higher in urban and semi-urban courts than in rural courts. However, in 1970 and also in 1971, the largest percentage increases in nonjudicial handling have been occurring in the rural courts, which reduces the gap in the proportion of cases handled nonjudicially by the smaller rural courts and the larger urban and semi-urban courts.[7]

Between 1970 and 1971 the number of delinquency cases handled judicially by all courts increased by only 1 per cent as contrasted with a 13 per cent increase in those handled nonjudicially. It is speculated that serious cases requiring judicial handling are leveling off or that with the recent emphasis on diverting juveniles at every stage of their involvement in the judicial system, a greater number of delinquency cases are being handled without the filing of a delinquency petition. When handled nonjudicially, the juvenile is most likely to have his case adjusted or referred to other community resources.

With the current increase of interest in and the development of juvenile diversionary programs throughout the Nation, not only after court referral but by the police and other institutions to community based programs, and other community . . . . one might speculate that this may continue to result in a decreasing number of juveniles handled by courts and subsequently committed to correctional institutions.[8] Allen F. Breed, Director, California Youth Authority, in the Foreword to their 1972 Annual Report states that the programs and activities of the Youth Authority during 1972 represents a year marked by a continuation of trends which began developing in the 1960's. These include declining commitments, increased emphasis on community-based programs, and older average age among those committed to the Department, and a continuing search for new and effective programs of rehabilitation, particularly among the growing number of offenders involved in drug abuse. He attributes the decline in commitment primarily due to the success of the Probation Subsidy program and the growth of community based programs for youthful offenders. At the same time, there has been a marked decline in parole revocations as a result of the Department's Increased Parole Effectiveness. As a result, two schools were closed in two years and it is planned to close a third institution in 1973.

The California's Youth Authority leadership role in youth development and delinquency prevention programs and projects is also described in the 1972 report.

Juvenile delinquency and the juvenile courts are presently under the critical scrutiny of social scientists and legislators. The President's Commission on Law Enforcement and Administration of Justice (Task Force Reports) all agree that the prevention of delinquency, the judicial handling of delinquent children, and the rehabilitation of these children present a multitude of unresolved problems. The Commission proposed the development of community services outside the juvenile court structure to deal with those children who present no serious danger to themselves or others, thereby allowing the court to concentrate its efforts on the more serious delinquent child. These services embrace what the Commission labeled the Youth Services Bureau; directed primarily toward those children whose conduct manifests the need for assistance but who have not committed acts which, if committed by an adult, would be a crime.[9]

The American Correctional Association in its publication "Juvenile Diversion, A Perspective" reports that in addition to the courts, police departments, schools, and youth service bureaus have played major roles in diversion programs. In Illinois, a variation of the police-administered diversion model is the Social Service Unit of the Wheaton Police Department begun in 1970 in Wheaton, Illinois with funding from the Illinois Law Enforcement Commission, a joint effort of the University of Illinois and the city police department. This report cites other examples of diversion programs as the Cook County Illinois Sheriff's Office, Youth Services Division. It states further that legislatures possess the greatest potential for expanding the utilization of diversionary alternatives to official processing for juvenile offenders. An example in this area is the new Illinois Unified Code of Corrections effective January 1974 which statute provides that no child under thirteen years of age shall be committed to the Illinois Department of Corrections. For other description of diversion programs reported the reader is referred to this publication as well as others cited below.[10] An example in this area is the new Illinois Unified Code of Corrections which in Article 5—Disposition in Amendments to the Juvenile Court Act, Section 705-2—Kinds of Disposition—states the following kinds of orders of disposition may be made in respect to wards of the court:

> (a) A minor found to be a delinquent under Section 2-2 may be (1) put on probation or conditional discharge and released to his parents, guardian or legal custodian, (2) placed in accordance with Section 5-7, with or without also being put on probation or conditional discharge, (3) where authorized under the "Drug Addiction Act", ordered admitted for treatment for drug addiction by the Department of Mental Health; (4) committed to the Department of Children and Family Services subject to Section 5 of "An Act creating the Department of Children and Family Services, codifying its powers and duties, and repealing certain Acts and Sections herein named"; or (5) committed to the Department of Corrections under Section 5-10, if he is 13 years of age or older, provided that minors less than 13 years of age may be

committed to the Department of Corrections until July 1, 1973. Thereafter, a minor less than 13 years of age may be committed to the Department of Corrections only upon certification by the Department of Children and Family Services that no fitting and proper placement is available or can be found for such minor and that the interests of society and the minor would best be served by his commitment to the Department of Corrections. Commitment to the Department of Corrections, Juvenile Division, shall be made only if a term of incarceration is permitted by law for adults found guilty of the offense for which the minor was adjudicated delinquent.[11]

REFERENCES

1. Annual Report—Program Description and Statistical Summary, Dept. of Youth Authority, Health and Welfare Agency, State of California, 1972, p. 28
2. Sussman, Frederick: *Law of Juvenile Delinquency*, 2nd ed., New York, Oceana, 1959, p. 21.
3. First Annual Report, 1970, Dept. of Correction, Printed by Authority of the State of Illnois, p. 20.
4. Annual Report, Dept. of the Youth Authority, Health and Welfare Agency, State of California, 1972, p. 22.
5. *Uniform Crime Reports*, Federal Bureau of Investigation, U. S. Department of Justice, Washington, D.C. 1972, pp. 137-159.
6. *Ibid*, p. 34.
7. "Juvenile Court Statistics—1971," U. S. Department of Health, Education and Welfare, Social and Rehabilitation Service, December 7, 1972, p. 3.
8. "Diverting Youth From the Correctional System," Dept. of Health, Education and Welfare, 1973, pp. 67-73.
9. President's Commission of Law Enforcement and Administration of Justice, *Task Force Report*, 1967, pp. 19-21.
10. "Juvenile diversion: A perspective: juvenile services project," *American Correctional Association*, July 1, 1972.
11. *Illinois Unified Code of Corrections*, St. Paul, West Publishing Company, July, 1972, p. 198.

APPENDIX A

As a follow-up research, the Institute for Juvenile Research[1] engaged in another research to briefly review the evidence of the past findings which showed a surprisingly higher incidence of misbehavior among adolescent girls in the past. These findings, with reference to an overview of the gender differences, used as a guideline the 36 specific types of adolescent misconduct about which the Illinois questionnaries had been concerned.

Table I is reproduced from this report and lists each of the 36 delinquent acts—for boys and girls separately—and the proportion of who committed each act more than once or twice.

Table I

ADOLESCENT MISBEHAVIORS AMONG BOYS AND GIRLS: ILLINOIS, 1972

Adolescent Misbehavior	Boys		Girls		Observed Differences	
	Ever	More Than Once or Twice	Ever	More Than Once or Twice	Ever	More Than Once or Twice
1. Cheated at school	73		74		+1	
		36		34		—2
2. Drank with permission	62		65		+3	
		38		65		+1
3. Drank without permission	62		60		—2	
		41		39		—2
4. Anonymous call	56		58		+2	
		29		30		+1
5. Petty theft	60		52		—8	
		20		18		—2
6. Shoplifting	54		47		—7	
		19		18		—1
7. Fistfight	64		37		—27	
		32		17		—15
8. Truancy	49		44		—5	
		26		22		—4
9. Got drunk	48		43		—5	
		30		26		—4
10. Driven without license or permit	50		37		—13	
		30		21		—9
11. Kept/used stolen goods	46		35		—11	
		17		14		—3
12. School fist fight	42		20		—22	
		—*		—*		—*
13. Driven too fast or recklessly	37		26		—11	
		18		11		—7

[1] A Note on Delinquency Involvement Among Adolescent Girls, Unpublished Report, Institute for Juvenile Research, funded by Illinois Law Enforcement Commission, 1973, p. 1.

14. Property damage	38	25	—13
	15	11	—4
15. Bothered teacher—thrown out of class	33	21	—12
	13	08	—5
16. Sexual intercourse	30	22	—8
	—*	—*	—*
17. Carried weapon	31	19	—12
	17	11	—6
18. Bought liquor	28	18	—10
	18	11	—7
19. Used marijuana	22	22	0
	13	14	+1
20. Runaway	22	22	0
	9	9	0
21. Gang fight	26	16	—10
	13	10	—3
22. Theft of $20	18	14	—4
	11	10	—1
23. Used weapon	18	13	—5
	11	10	—1
24. Breaking and entering	15	11	—4
	11	9	—2
25. Strongarming	15	11	—4
	10	9	—1
26. Bet on sports event	16	7	—8
	—*	—*	—*
27. Joyriding	11	8	—3
	7	6	—1
28. Bet on policy game	12	7	—5
	—*	—*	—*
29. Stripped car	11	6	—5
	8	5	—3
30. Used psychedelics	8	8	0
	4	5	+1
31. Used downers	7	9	+2
	4	5	+1
32. Used uppers	8	9	+1
	4	5	+1
33. Used inhalants	8	6	—2
	4	3	—1
34. Sold drugs	6	5	—1
	3	3	0
35. Used heroin	3	3	0
	2	2	0
36. Used microzine	3	3	0
	2	2	0

For persons ever committing each act, the 36 items in the table[2] can be summarized as follows:

> Girls more often involved than boys (margin less than 10%)—5 items
>
> No observed difference between boys and girls—5 items
>
> Boys more often involved than girls (margin less than 10%)—16 items

[2] Ibid, p. 1-3.

Boys more often involved than girls (10% margin or more)—
    10 items

For all but 10 of the delinquency items a difference of less than 10 per cent separates the responses of boys and girls. The modal response category (involving 16 items) shows boys as being moderately more involved in delinquent acts. For ten of the items, there is either no boy-girl difference at all in delinquency involvement, or only a modest margin favoring girls.

Gender differences are most pronounced in the area of personal violence. These items include fistfights, carrying weapons and gangfights. These activities are very much male-dominated, although even here, the rates for girls might strike some observers as rather high.

Automobile violations follow the same pattern: boys have a distinct edge, but the incidence of traffic violations among girls is not negligible. Certain property violations (keeping/using stolen goods and vandalism) also fit this description.

✓ Finally, there seem to be no substantial gender differences at all in the area of drug use.

The report states that the reaction to these figures was one of mild surprise. It had been expected to uncover more gender difference, and more substantial gender differences than the table revealed. The report further states that the expectations were guided primarily by knowledge of the literature on official rates (police and court statistics) whose figures often reveal that boys with three to five offenses are more likely than girls to be designated as juvenile offenders. Recollection of earlier self-report studies of delinquent behavior by the IJR Project Director revealed more substantial gender differences than uncovered in Illinois.

✓ In systematically reviewing earlier self-report surveys in the pattern of female delinquency with the 1972 Illinois report, the results are that girls tend to report a higher level of misbehavior than they have reported in the past.

APPENDIX B

A California Youth Authority Girl:
Juvenile Court First Commitment

Her Home Environment

1. Sixty-one per cent came from a below average socio-economic environment with 35 per cent from an environment judged to be average and 4 per cent above average.
2. A significant number (37%) came from homes where all or part of the family income was from public assistance, but the majority (63%) came from homes which were economically self-supporting.
3. Forty-nine per cent had been placed in one or more foster homes while 15 per cent had experienced one or more contacts of a dependency nature.

Her Family

1. Sixty-five per cent had parents who were not living together at the time of commitment either due to divorce or separation (52%) or death (13%).
2. Forty-four per cent had one or both parents who had completed high school. For the remaining 56 per cent, neither parent had completed high school.
3. Sixty-six per cent had fathers or father substitutes with no known criminal record.

Her Schooling

1. Attitude toward school was judged to be positive in only 20 per cent of the cases while in the remaining 80 per cent it was judged to be indifferent or negative.
2. Seventy-three per cent had been involved in serious school misbehavior on more than an occasional basis. Only 4 per cent had no record of serious school misbehavior.
3. The last school grade enrolled in prior to commitment was at the junior high school level, grades 7-9 (35%), or the senior high school level, grades 10-12 (64%).
4. Achievement test scores place her at the seventh grade level in arithmetic. Her reading comprehension and vocabulary scores are at the eighth grade level.

Her Developmental Behavior

1. Her intelligence level as tested by nonverbal instruments give her an I.Q. of 93.
2. No evidence has been shown of a serious psychological disorder (54%).
3. Ninety per cent had friends who tended to a delinquent orientation. Only 4 per cent had friends who were mainly nondelinquent.
4. Fifty-nine per cent stated Protestantism as their religious belief while 40 per cent were Catholics, although many had only fragmentary contact with a religious heritage.

Her Delinquent Behavior

1. Eighty-seven per cent had three or more delinquent contacts prior to being committed to the Youth Authority. Only 1 per cent had no prior delinquent contacts.
2. Sixty-nine per cent had no prior commitments to a juvenile institution while 26 per cent had one and 5 per cent had two or more prior commitments.
3. The majority (89%) had not used weapons in either their past or present offenses.
4. The majority (89%) did not have the use of alcohol associated with either their present offense or any past offenses.
5. Thirty-two per cent had co-offenders in the commission of their present offense.
6. Only 15 per cent had no known narcotic history. Sixty-two per cent had used marijuana or dangerous drugs while 22 per cent had used opiates.
7. The median age at the time of first delinquent contact was 13.9 years.

CHAPTER 2

SOME THEORETICAL CONCEPTS

THE TERM "JUVENILE DELINQUENCY" has no universal definition
in common with offenses leading to commitment. In New
Mexico, a child is a delinquent who "habitually" refuses to obey
his parents, or who is "habitually" wayward, disobedient or un-
controlled. How often may a child perform an act before it is
considered "habitual"? A Massachusetts law defines a juvenile
delinquent as "a child between seven and seventeen who violates
any city ordinance or town bylaw or who commits an offense not
punishable by death." Under this law, nearly every child in the
state within this age range is, or will be, delinquent by definition.
For instance, Professor Charles W. Coulter points out that an
eight-year-old girl who lights a firecracker to celebrate the fourth
of July could be considered delinquent, hence the term "delinquency" is vague.[1]

Bloch and Flynn prefer the British common-law definition of
delinquency, namely, "any act that, if committed by an adult,
would be considered criminal".[2] Sophia M. Robinson states that
"delinquency" is an umbrella term for a wide variety of socially
disapproved behavior varying with time, place and administrative
attitudes. Delinquency is any behavior which a given community
at a given time is considered in conflict with its best interests,
whether or not the offender has been brought into court.[3]

Leo J. Trese defines "delinquency" as "any repetitive behavior
on the part of an adolescent girl of normal intelligence, behavior
which is contrary to law, does exhibit a breakdown of the ego in
its management of impulse."[4] "Juvenile delinquency is not a disease
or a clinical entity. It is a descriptive term referring to a high area
of a social and antisocial behavior. In most juvenile research, the

19

phrase "juvenile delinquent" denotes a child who has been offici-
ally acted upon by the courts, the adjudicated delinquent.[5]

According to Jerome S. Weiss, juvenile delinquency is generally
thought of in social or psychological terms but seldom in legal
terms. It has been defined as "a child trying to act like a grown-
up." Actually, delinquency is a "legal" concept, and a delinquent
is "what the law says it is".[6]

The first juvenile delinquency law, passed by the State of
Illinois in 1899, illustrates the magnitude of the problem of definition regarding juvenile delinquency as well as the futility of
an omnibus type of law. Sociologist Ruth S. Cavan quotes the
former Illinois statutes:[7]

> "Delinquent Child" defined. Sec. 1. Be it enacted by the People
> of the State of Illinois, represented by the General Assembly:
> That for the purposes of this Act a delinquent child is any male
> who while under the age of 17 years, or any female who while
> under the age of 18 years, violates any law of this State; or is
> incorrigible, or knowingly associates with thieves, vicious or
> immoral persons; or without just cause and without the consent
> of its parents, guardian or custodian absents itself from its home
> or place of abode, or is growing up in idleness or crime; or
> knowingly frequents a house of ill repute; or knowingly fre-
> quents any policy shop or place where any gambling device is
> operated; or frequents any saloon or dram shop where intoxi-
> cating liquors are sold; or patronizes or visits any public pool
> room or bucket shop; or wanders about any railroad yards or
> tracks or jumps or attempts to jump onto any moving train; or
> habitually wanders about the streets in the nighttime without
> being on any lawful business or lawful occupation; or enters
> any car or engine without lawful authority; or uses vile, ob-
> scene, vulgar or indecent language in any public place or about
> any school house; or is guilty of indecent or lascivious conduct.

Definitions of "delinquency," the delinquent herself and even
the offenses are frequently vague, stilted, quaint, inconsistent or
mutually exclusive. In the United States, there are too many
purely moral judgments such as "willful disobedience," "incorrigibility," "stubbornness," "associating with vicious persons," and
similar terms upon which there can be no general agreement.
Hence, the offenses leading to commitment tend to be merely
descriptive of the unlawful behavior and lacking any consistency in

meaning and interpretation from state to state, even when the same terminology defining the offense is employed.

The delinquency statutes were originally designed to be protective. But the public now attaches a stigma to delinquency as it does to criminality. Today, even the word "juvenile," the Latin word for "young," through its long association with the word "delinquency" has acquired unfavorable connotations.

There seem to be as many causes of juvenile delinquency as there are individuals who have studied the problem. As Lejins has indicated, the search for causes of juvenile delinquency is apt to be disappointing. A lifetime is not long enough to familiarize oneself with all the writing available on the subject of juvenile delinquency and criminality. Moreover, the great mass of research on this subject appears to be in a state of confusion.[8]

Proponents of the biological or constitutional approach to an explanation of delinquency and crime were among the very first to appear in the literature. According to them, the delinquent was possessed of evil spirits, a born criminal (born biological type) or a moron. Lombroso, the "putative father of the constitutional approach" and founder of the typological schools which stressed the thesis that "criminals differ physically from non-criminals," contributed such concepts as the "atavistic character, physical deficiency and criminal stigmata" of the offender. Exner noted the "inherited proneness toward delinquency" and Lange found inheritance significant in his studies of criminal twins. Kretschmer's "pyknic, athletic and asthenic" body-mind types approach to delinquency was further refined by Sheldon's "endomorphic, mesomorphic and ectomorphic" body-mind types. Frey, Exner's disciple, analyzed the cases of 160 youths in trouble over a twenty-six year span and concluded that a "familial predisposition" was largely responsible for delinquent behavior. The Gluecks' concept of "criminal maturation" stressed biological attributes, and the delinquent boy who emerged from their study has been dubbed the "mesomorphic delinquent." Goddard stressed the mentally deficient character of the delinquent while Hooton, one of the more recent of the neo-Lombrosians, stressed the "biological inferiority" of those who violate the law. These researchers tended to reflect the point of view of the European biological school of criminality, which has found some acceptance in South America with anthropologists on many prison staffs and in clinics.

According to Reckless,[9] the behaviorial scientists of the United States would not accept the close relationship of delinquency to athletic physique, in spite of Glueck's findings relative to the mesomorphic somatotype. Sociologists in the United States believe that sex and age roles have as much to do with delinquency as do the biological components of maleness and young adulthood. They also believe that the psychopathic personality is not a definite personality entity inherited through the family strain as had been indicated by Kurt Schneider, an Austrian psychiatrist.

Proponents of the psychiatric and psychogenic approach to delinquency have attempted to separate character and personality from physique and heredity. The main criminal predisposition which psychoanalysts describe is the inability to control impulses. Accordingly, the criminal carries out in his actions his natural unbridled instinctual drives; he acts as the child would act if it only could.[10] Hertha Tarrasch states that there is a "delinquency potential in every child, hence delinquency is almost normal behavior." She believes that the delinquent does not differ from the noncriminal in his basic makeup. Rather, we are all born with antisocial needs but, as a result of parental training, most of us develop effective checks for these impulses; the delinquent does not. The delinquent has a weak ego or one whose effectiveness is reduced by emotional conflict.[11]

Among the earlier contributors to the psychogenic theories was Aichhorn, who in his *Wayward Youth* (1925), opined that "some children linger on as aggrandizing infants, living on the pleasure principle instead of developing a reality principle of life."[12] Friedlander, (1947) noted "antisocial character formation" as a result of a disturbed ego-development during the first three years of life—the three-year old cannot stand tension and may react with neurotic or delinquent behavior.[13] Redl, in his *Children Who Hate* (1951) with David Wineman, believed that these children fail to develop a management system and develop a delinquent ego, an ego which is guilt free, and enjoys delinquency. Redl defined vandalism as "group psychological intoxication" that hides much hatred and aggression. He theorized that many children who resort to vandalism have not had a single warm relationship with an adult.[14]

There has been a substantial amount of revealing research regarding the emotional life of delinquents. One of the most significant and thorough studies was conducted by Healy and Bronner. They found that "no less than 91 per cent of the delinquents gave clear evidence of being or having been very unhappy and discontented in their life circumstances, or extremely disturbed because of emotional-provoking situations or experiences." Similar evidence of inner stresses was found at most in only 13 per cent of the control group. Slawson, Burt, Carr and the Gluecks stressed and substantiated the findings of Healy and Bronner. The emotional disturbances within delinquents have been categorized by Healy and Bronner as "feelings of being rejected, insecure, not understood in affectional relationships; deep feelings of being thwarted; feelings of inadequacies or inferiority in homes, school groups, etc; intense feelings of discomfort about family disharmonies; feelings of jealousy, or being discriminated against; feelings of confused unhappiness; a conscious or unconscious sense of guilt in regard to their behavior."[15]

Healy's fundamental work, *The Individual Delinquent*, led to a present-day examination of the individual offender. This modern research, associated with the names of Healy and his collaborators, Burk, Aichhorn, Alexander, Skaub and others, undoubtedly shows that the differences in the psychological makeup of the delinquent and the nondelinquent are quantitative rather than qualitative.[16]

Freud, Aichhorn and Alexander, psychoanalysts who were interested in the personality of the criminal, started their research with a knowledge of the workings of both the normal and the disturbed mind.[17] Psychoanalysis discovered that the roots of unconscious tendencies which influence our actions go back to experiences of early childhood. It had shown that the actions of normal persons and still more obviously those of neurotic persons, could be understood if their unconscious motivations were taken into account.

Jerome B. Bates indicates that those of psychiatric orientation are critical of efforts to fix the etiology of delinquency in such social factors as "the broken home," "habits of thought," "incompetent or indifferent parents," "evil associates," and "inadequate supervision." Experiences, particularly those which were once charged with painful emotion and have since been repressed, are of special importance in understanding motivations of delinquency.[18]

In the opinion of a psychiatrist, Dr. David Abrahamsen, delinquency and crime are products of a person's tendencies and the situation of the moment interacting with his mental resistance. Abrahamsen stresses that some children become predisposed to aggression due to childhood emotional deprivation. The offender seldom turns to delinquency overnight, but gradually becomes sensitized to delinquent activities. More psychosomatic disorders, e.g. enuresis, are found among delinquents than among nondelinquents.[19]

Leontine R. Young directs attention to the fact that juvenile delinquents are children whom far too many in authority have forgotten. Behind the delinquency, behind the mask is a hurt and miserable child, twisted by violence, stunned by hate and blinded by fear. As adults, our concern is not for the child but for his behavior. We proceed on the naive premise that a delinquent child is simply "bad" because he wants to be, because he enjoys being that way. Unless children are respected as individuals, not much respect for adults may be anticipated.[20]

As McDavid and McCandless point out so well, adolescence is a period of crisis in the socialization process because it is too prolonged. The adolescent is denied the protection of childhood, denied the rewards of adulthood and, psychosocially, is in a "no-man's land.[21]

In contrast to the biological and psychogenic approaches to juvenile delinquency, sociological research has emphasized the many environmental factors which contribute to delinquency. Investigation of such factors as the broken home, lack of discipline, bad companions, lack of organized leisure time and economic conditions, in conjunction with modern psychological research, has caused the shifting of emphasis from the punishment of the offender to the examination of the social conditions which have produced the juvenile delinquent's antisocial personality.[22]

Ferri denied the freewill doctrine and the "moral responsibility" of Beccaria, the "Father of Criminology," and called attention to "bad environment" as being more significant to delinquency. Garofalo noted that natural crimes, e.g. murder, rape, robbery, arson, and assault, violated the two basic altruistic sentiments of pity and probity. Durkheim's "anomie" helps individuals (into delinquency) as they drift without meaningful social ties (into misbehavior). The social facts of delinquency are our only clue to reality; it is the social reaction to the act, not the act itself, which determines whether or not it is criminal behavior. (Tarde's "imitation and suggestion" theory holds that crime goes in waves from one community to another.) Bonger stressed that the "exchange" part of the economic system depersonalizes human relationships, and delinquency is caused by greed and envy which would occur even if everyone had a good job. Sullenger's "mobility" theory of delinquency suggests that towns with transient populations have higher delinquency rates. Sellin's "culture conflict" theory concludes that delinquency may develop in marginal personalities due to differences in beliefs, morals, manners, language and ideals. Taft stressed the "materialistic, arrogant culture patterns" which tend to produce delinquency. Tannenbaum emphasized "community" which generates as much delinquency as we deserve, and that delinquency is as eternal as society and is as much a part of our culture as sickness, disease or death. We cannot change or reduce delinquency without changing our way of life.

Clifford R. Shaw found in his Chicago study that rates of delinquent males and delinquent females taken before the juvenile court varied by square mile areas from 0.8 to 19.4 (boys) and 0.1 to 9 (girls) per one hundred persons, ten to sixteen years of age. A certain consistency in the variations of delinquency from area to area was noted.[23] In a comparative study of twenty-one cities, Shaw and

McKay noted that in each city the areas of highest delinquency had the same characteristics.[24] In a previous study, Shaw and McKay indicated that areas of highest delinquency rates also were areas of declining population, physical deterioration and concentration of foreign-born and black population.[25] The studies of Shaw, Carr and Thurston agree with most sociologists that a concentration of delinquents is found in the slums. Delinquency is believed to be a function of an area.

Sutherland's "differential association" theory stresses that delinquency is learned like school lessons, usually from primary group instruction in association with others, depending upon the frequency, intensity, priority and duration of contacts. Glaser's "differential identification" theory indicates that the delinquent may identify with real or imaginary persons without necessarily associating with them. Quetelet, the first "social criminologist" inaugurated the geographic school of criminology, stressing maps, surveys, statistics and ecological techniques. The subsequent neographic school was represented by Lindesmith, Shaw, McKay, Park and Burgess.

Cohen, following the lead suggested by Whyte's *Street Corner Society* that delinquents find their status in the subculture of the gang, stated that much lower-class delinquency is nonutilitarian, malicious and negativistic, based on "short-run hedonism, a working-class reaction to fate," Lower-class youth is unable to compete with middle-class youth.[26] According to Parsons, however, some delinquency is a phenomenon of the middle-class norms. Middle-class children are isolated from adult males. The females handle the discipline and set the standards of good conduct in both home and school. Hence, the middle-class boy unconsciously identifies "goodness" with feminity, and may become a "bad boy" just to play a "male" role.[27]

After studying 1,313 gangs containing 25,000 members concentrated around Chicago's Loop, Thrasher concluded that gangs characteristically are found in geographically and socially interstitial areas. Bloch and Niederhoffer state that the gang is an unintended consequence of modern, multi-ethnic, industrialized urban living and hence not explained in terms of a struggle between social classes.

According to Sykes and Matza, delinquent activities of the lower class are similar to leisure activities of the middle classes, but lower-class persons get into trouble due to their poor sense of timing and appropriateness. Delinquent girls in lower classes do not reject middle-class standards. They know that promiscuity is "wrong," but it is often expected of them. Delinquency appears to be attractive to youths engaged in a restless search for excitement, verbal and physical aggression, and who have a disdain for occupational goals.[28] Reiss and Rhodes state that peer-oriented delinquency is the most common form of delinquent organization at both status levels, but the career-oriented delinquent is found only among lower-class youth.[29]

Tappan points out that the official designation, "delinquent," implies involvement with the police, detention, court handling, correctional treatment and a resulting role and stigma that are ineradicably injurious, despite idyllic euphemisms to the contrary.[30] According to Neumeyer, juvenile delinquency should be viewed as a social problem and is sufficiently widespread to require concerted social action on the national, state and local basis.[31]

Although there are many theories of delinquency, there have emerged some fairly clear concepts of causes related to this challenging problem. Adelaide M. Johnson, psychiatrist,[32] concludes that the central causation as viewed by many students today indicates two large categories of antisocial behavior—the unconsciously driven individual delinquent from the so-called "good" or "normal" family, and the gang or sociologic group operating at any economic level. There is overlapping of these two large groups. What operates casually in the individual delinquent is to a large extent different from what propels the gang or sociologic form of delinquency and this in turn dictates different treatment measures for the two groups.

The individual delinquent frequently suffers from neurotic guilt. Resolution is sought in acting-out conflicts. There is defective superego structure which includes the overwhelming, parentally determined, dynamic push toward antisocial behavior which the child senses and with which he necessarily complies. The antisocial acting-out in a child is unconsciously fostered and sanctioned by the parents who vicariously achieve gratification of their own poorly integrated, forbidden impulses through a child's acting-out. In turn, the child's behavior stimulates the parents to added need for this gratification.

The "social disorganization" theories maintain that sociologic delinquency flourishes in the intercity area of large cities, not only where the area is economically depressed but also where the population is mobile and never achieves a solidarity of community spirit or social organization. Some authors maintain that the adult world presents no clear-cut, authoritative models to the child, and he is confused and lacking in respect for any code. Other authors maintain that there is in this group a subculture unity with codes, but it is incongruent with the larger society. The gangs or subculture groups from which they stem may have little guilt about stealing from or manhandling those outside their culture.

The principle conclusion of research by Shaw, McKay and their associates[33] was that sociologic delinquency is a subcultural tradition in the areas of the city inhabited by the lower socioeconomic classes. Such delinquent groups were not correlated with any national group. However, at no time did Shaw and McKay maintain that economic factors were the whole answer to the problem. Although sociologic delinquents were likely to come from lower-class homes, that is not to say that gang delinquency does not arise in upper-class areas.

Many authors feel that a multiplicity of variables enter the picture in sociologic delinquency, with no single one asserting itself as the specific stimulus. Not only do clashes of class and poverty enter. There is child neglect, lack of consistent supervision, adult antisocial example and all degrees of rejection and cruelty—all creating their own personality problems, the solution to which may be sought in identification with common problems of the gang.

It is important to emphasize that a variety of theories of delinquency arise because there are a variety of kinds of delinquents. Marquerite Q. Warren[34] stresses the fact that delinquents differ from each other not only in the form of their delinquency but also in the reasons for and meaning of their delinquency. Some individuals are delinquent because the peer group on which they depend for approval prescribes delinquent behavior as the price of acceptance, or because the values which they have internalized are those of a deviant subculture. Other individuals are delinquent because of insufficient socialization, while still others are delinquently acting out internal conflicts, identity struggles or family crises.

✓Juvenile gangs reflect the social structure of the community, both in their frequency and the type of behavior in which their members engage. A quarter of a century ago, Frederic M. Thrasher[35] made an impressive contribution to the understanding of juvenile gangs. Thrasher observed that the "gang represents the efforts of boys to create a society for themselves where none adequate to their needs exists." Of course, all gangs do not engage in delinquent activities. But, the activities of delinquent gangs in large cities have created serious problems.

Girls in delinquent gangs seem to play special and subordinated roles. Some are recruited, others become members voluntarily, while still others enter only under threats of physical violence. Sometimes the membership of these female auxiliaries is indicated by secret symbols such as a spider tatooed on the left hand, attesting affiliation with "The Spiders" of Los Angeles. Or the girls may have designs carved on themselves, especially if they are defined by the boys as subsidiary members.

The girls are often expected to submit to the sexual advances of the male members. They sometimes assist boys in gang fights by concealing weapons, e.g. knives and fingernail files. As illustrated a few years ago, they concealed these weapons in the then popular high pompadour arrangements of their hair. Girls have been used by male gangs to waylay leaders of rival groups—the traditional "decoy" technique. These seem to be the principal activities of even those girls who organize their own female gangs such as the "Shangrila-Debs," "Robinettes" and others. William Bernard summarizes as follows:

Only rarely does the girl gang function without affiliation. In the great majority of cases, it exists as the auxiliary of some boy

gang, to which it gives fierce loyalty. One important duty is to
act as weapon carriers for the boys, who thus escape seizure and
charges. The girls also supply alibis, claiming that a suspect boy
was with her at a "session," or in bed at the time of the crime's
occurrence. Principally, however, the young ladies act as camp
followers, supplying the lads with such sex as they require and
fulfilling duties as lures and spies.[36]

Although youth gangs, like delinquency, are not restricted to any
racial or ethnic group, those operating in the nation's black
ghettos are a matter of major concern. Phyl Garland states:

> These names reflect the stunted values of the ravaged com-
> munities that spawned them—Vice Lords, Hornets, Cobras,
> Dusters, Imperial Pimps. They range in size from the causal
> knots of youngsters who merely hang together in their own
> "hood" to Chicago's Mighty Blackstone Rangers, Inc., who esti-
> mate their membership at 1,500 and are currently considered
> one of the largest and best organized youth gangs in the country.
> With their violent past, hopeful present and unpredictable fu-
> ture, the Rangers exemplify both the best and the worst of the
> gang phenomenon. . . . They acquired a "ladies auxiliary" called
> the Blackstone Rangeretts and extended their influence into
> neighboring middle-class South areas.[37]

The Chicago Police Department, which considers the city's gang
problem to be of great concern, has set up a special Gang Intelligence unit within the Detective Division.

The idea of juvenile delinquency was pointed out as a "cover"
for many youthful predaceous activities. The female delinquent
may compound problems, due to age differentials. In some areas,
the upper age limit for treating girls as delinquents is 18 years. For
boys this limit is 16 years. Such "reverse sexism" seems to ignore
the fact that girls mature earlier than boys. In Alberta, Canada,
one sixteen-year-old boy was convicted of contributing to juvenile
delinquency and sentenced to a short term in the Fort Saskatche-
wan gaol. His 'offense' was that he was guilty of having sexual intercourse with his steady girl friend, a young woman who was nearly
eighteen.[38]

Juveniles may be affected by "certain acts committed by school
people" and some have proposed that such acts be labeled "criminal" if cruelty to children is involved, and charging the teacher or

administrator with being an accessory to whatever crime the child commits in later life.

A popular hypothesis concerning youthful robbery is that it may be "nasty, but not serious." As reported by Gwynn Nettler, in his *Explaining Crime,* as measured by the Selling and Wolfgang Index, this hypothesis was contradicted by the finding that "seriousness per juvenile event . . . is consistently greater . . . than for all robbery events taken together."[40]

Nettler summarizes the possibility of juveniles being arrested, that arrest is an interactional process, that official records reflect the operation of a judicial sieve. There is little prejudice in the judicial system. Nettler quotes studies by various investigators, as Weiner and Willie who examined decisions of juvenile officers in search of racial or class bias. They found no such effect.[41] As regards police discretion, "police powers seem to reside, for better or worse, in the hands of the people."

Most juvenile delinquency remains hidden. The imperfections of official statistics on delinquency have led investigators to think of other ways of measuring offenses. As indicated by Nettler, these unofficial procedures would include (1) direct observations of delinquent activity, (2) surveys of the victims of delinquency, and (3) studies of confessions of delinquency. Many studies produce inconsistencies, due to unreliability and invalidity in questionnaires and interviews. Words and phrases many mean different things, memories are often inaccurate, responses can vary according to emotionality of subject matter, even personality traits of both the one interviewed and the interrogator.[43]

In juvenile delinquency, ethnic differences are real differences. The "melting pot" theory more often expresses hope rather than fact.[44] As Nettler concludes, in his effort to count delinquency and crime, "we are all subject to temptation, and given the right (or wrong) combination of opportunity, pressure, need, and passion, even an improbable crime may become part of our fate. Nettler quotes Tolstoy's humanistic dictum that 'the seeds of every crime are in each of us' but holds that the seeds are germinated under different conditions that raise or lower the probability of their fruition."[45]

REFERENCES

1. Coulter, Charles W.: *Federal Probation. XII*: 14, Sept. 1948.
2. Bloch, Herbert A., and Flyn, Frank T.: *Delinquency: The Juvenile Offender in America Today.* New York, Random, 1956, p. 7.
3. Robison, Sophia M.: *Juvenile Delinquency: Its Nature and Control.* New York, Holt, 1960, pp. 3-11.
4. Trese, Leo J.: *101 Delinquent Girls.* Notre Dame, Fides, 1962, p. 5.
5. Vedder, Clyde B.: *Juvenile Offenders.* Springfield, Thomas, 1963, p. 4.
6. Weiss, Jerome S.: Criminals or delinquents? Another Illinois merry-go-round! *Chicago Bar Record,* Jan. 1953, p. 2.
7. Cavan, Ruth S.: *Juvenile Delinquency.* Philadelphia, Lippincott, 1969, p. 24.
8. Lejins, Peter: Pragmatic etiology of delinquent behavior. *Social Forces, 29*:317-320, March 1951.
9. Reckless, Walter: *The Crime Problem,* 3rd ed. New York, Appleton, 1967, p. 383.
10. Tarrasch, Herta: Delinquency in normal behavior. *Focus, 29*:97-101, July 1950.
11. Toch, Hans, and Goldstein, Jacob: The development of criminal predispositions. In Toch, Hans, (Ed): *Legal and Criminal Psychology.* New York, Holt, 1961, p. 207.
12. Aichorn, A.: *Wayward Youh,* 2nd ed. New York, Viking, 1955.
13. Friedlander, Kate: *The Psycho-Analytical Approach to Juvenile Delinquency.* New York, *Int Univ Pr,* 1947.
14. Redl, Fritz, and Wineman, David: *Children Who Hate.* Glencoe, Free Pr, 1951.
15. Mihanovich, Clement S.: Who is the juvenile delinquent? *Social Science 22* (No.2):145-149, April 1947.
16. Friedlander, Kate: op. cit., pp. 5-9.
17. Ibid, p. 10.
18. Bates, Jerome E.: Abrahamsen's theory of the etiology of criminal acts. *The Journal of Criminal Law and Criminology, XL*:471-475, Dec. 1949.
19. Abrahamsen, David: *The Psychology of Crime.* New York, Columbia U P, 1960, p 37.
20. Young, Leontine R.: We call them delinquents. *Federal Probation, XV*:9-13, Dec. 1951.
21. Psychological aspects of delinquency. *Journal of Criminal Law, Criminology and Police Science, 53*:1-14, March 1962.
22. Friedlander, Kate: op. cit., p. 6.
23. Shaw, Clifford R., *et al.*: *Delinquency Areas.* Chicago, U of Chicago Pr, 1929, pp. 38-152.

24. Shaw, Clifford R., and McKay, Henry D.: *Juvenile Delinquency and Urban Areas.* Chicago, U Chicago Pr, 1942, pp. 435-437.
25. Shaw, Clifford R., and McKay, Henry D.: Social factors in juvenile delinquency. National Commission of Law Observance and Enforcement Report of the Causes of Crime. Washington, 1931, vol. 2, 60-108.
26. Cohen, Albert K.: *Delinquent Boys: The Culture of the Gang.* Glencoe, Free Pr, 1955.
27. Parsons, Talcott: Certain primary sources and patterns of aggression in the social structure of the western world. *Psychiatry,* 10:172, May 1947.
28. Matza, David, and Sykes, Gresham M.: Juvenile delinquency and subterranean values. American Sociological Review, 26:712-713, Oct. 1961.
29. Reiss, Albert J., Jr., and Rhodes, Albert Lewis: The distribution of juvenile delinquency in the social class structure. *Am Sociol Rev,* 26:720-732, Oct. 1961.
30. Tappan, Paul W.: *Juvenile Delinquency.* New York, McGraw-Hill, 1949, p. 4.
31. Neumeyer, Martin H.: *Juvenile Delinquency in Modern Society.* Princeton, Van Nostrand, 1961, p. 4.
32. Johnson, Dr. Adelaide M.: Juvenile delinquency. In Arieti, S. (Ed): *American Handbook of Psychiatry.* New York, Basic Books, 1959, vol. I, pp. 841-855.
33. Shaw, Clifford R., and McKay, Henry D.: Social factors in juvenile delinquency. National Commission on Law Enforcement Report on Causes of Crime, Washington, D.C., 1931, vol. II.
34. Warren, Marguerite Q.: The Community Treatment Project: An Integration of Theories of Causation and Correctional Practice. Presented at the Annual Conference of the Illinois Academy of Criminology, Chicago, Illinois, May 14, 1965.
35. Vedder, Clyde B.: *Juvenile Offenders.* Springfield, Thomas, 1969, pp. 104-116.
36. Bernard, William: *Jailbait.* New York, Greenberg, 1949, p. 93. For an excellent discussion of girl gangs in New York see Hanson, Kitty: *Rebels in the Streets.* Englewood Cliffs, P-H, 1964.
37. Garland, Phyl: The gang phenomenon: big city headache. *Ebony Magazine,* Aug. 1967, pp. 96-103.
38. Cousineau, D. F., and Veevers, J. E.: Juvenile justice: an analysis of the Canadian young offenders act. In Boydell, C. *et al,* (Eds): *Deviant Behavior and Societal Reaction.* Toronto, H, R & W, 1972.
39. Thomas, A.: Community power and student rights. *Harvard Educational Review,* 42:173-216, May, 1972.

40. Nettler, Gwynn: *Explaining Crime,* New York, McGraw, 1974.
41. Weine, N. L., and Willie, C. V.: Decision by juvenile officers. *Am J Sociol, 77*:199-210, Sept. 1971.
42. Hagen, J. L.: The labelling perspective, the delinquent, and the police. A review of the literature. *Canadian Journal of Criminology and Corrections, 14*:150-165, April 1972.
43. Haber, R. N.: How we remember what we see. *Scientific American, 222*:104-112, May 1970.
44. Novak, M.: *The Rise of the Unmeltable Ethnics.* New York Macmillan.
45. Nettler, *op. cit.,* pp. 88-97.

CHAPTER 3

THE AREA OF FEMALE
DELINQUENCY AND CRIME

THERE HAS BEEN A PAUCITY of published research in the area of *female delinquency* and crime. Most studies have concerned themselves with *male delinquency* and criminality, since males predominate in crime by about five to one at the juvenile training-school level and by nearly thirty to one at the adult prison level.

The pioneer research on the female offender was done by ✓ Lombroso just prior to 1900. This Italian anthropologist and physician contended that the female offender, including the prostitute, was less likely to be a born criminal type than the male offender and was more likely to display the characteristics of an "occasional" offender, who today might be termed a "situational offender" or an "offender of opportunity." Her "reluctant crime" may have originated in the suggestion of a lover, husband, father or even a female companion. Lombroso cited parental neglect and desertion as highly causative factors leading to early female theft and prostitution.[1]

Another important female-offender study was made in 1920 by Mabel Fernwald, who used the inmates (mostly prostitutes) of the New York Reformatory for Women in her sample. This study presented no theory. It merely emphasized the women's impoverished backgrounds: limited schooling, employment at an early age, meager industrial training and a relatively inferior mentality.[2]

In 1923, in a less factual but more systematic way, William Issac Thomas viewed the sexually delinquent girl as an "unadjusted" girl, somewhat on the amoral side, who, by using sex as capital, attempts to satisfy her dominant wishes for security, recognition, new experience and response. Thomas postulated that human motives could be reduced to these four basic wishes, generated by the social circumstances and personalized by the individual's definition of the situation. In his view the wishes are, for the most part, on the conscious level.[3]

Sheldon and Eleanor Glueck did research in 1934 on female offenders, assembling casefolder data on a consecutive sample of five hundred Massachusetts Reformatory for Women inmates. The Gluecks' research did not proceed on the basis of testing any theory or hypothesis about the female offender. It did, however, single out five factors bearing the highest association to nonrecidivism: (a) retardation in school, (b) neighborhood influences with a year of commitment, (c) steadiness of employment (d) economic responsibility and (e) mental abnormality. In their *Five Hundred Delinquent Women,* the Gluecks characterized their sample as a "swarm of defective, diseased, antisocial misfits which a reformatory and a parole system are required by society to transform into wholesome, decent, law-abiding citizens.[4]

In 1943, Tage Kemp summarized case histories of 530 Copenhagen clinic-treated prostitutes, finding them socially, medically and psychologically below par. He believed that depressed social, physical and psychological conditions plunged these women into prostitution.[5]

✓A more recent definitive study on the female offender was undertaken by Otto Pollak in 1950. He attempted a systematic explanation of why female criminality was so much less frequently reported than male criminal behavior. Pollak found that female criminality was especially under-reported in such areas as shoplifting, thefts by prostitutes, thefts by domestic servants, abortions, perjury, disturbance of the peace, offenses against children and homicide. He also noted that offenses such as homosexuality and exhibitionism go practically undetected if committed by women. In his *The Criminality of Women,* Pollack points out that the woman's public image as homemaker, child rearer, nurse, mistress and other related roles puts her in a good position to commit and screen her crimes from public view. Female criminality is largely masked criminality, as women use deceit and indirection in committing their offenses. The real measure of female criminality must be sought from unofficial sources.[6]

In his *Delinquent Boys: The Culture of the Gang* (1955), Albert K. Cohen commented on the female delinquent in his analysis of the delinquent male subculture. It is implicit in his theory that the female delinquent is likely to be involved in delinquency simply because of her adjustment to males, since the bulk of her behavior is sex-connected, unlike the stealing and malicious hell-raising of her male counterpart.[7]

The "occasional offender" theory of Lombroso, the "wish satisfaction" theory of Thomas, the "masked behavior" theory of Pollak and the "boy's girl" theory of Cohen represent the principal attempts to explain criminality. However, since 1955 additional attempts have been made to clarify the social significance and implications of female criminality.

In their *New Horizons In Criminology* (1959),[8] Barnes and Teeters reject the thesis that women commit fewer crimes than men because they are inherently more moral and innocuous. Women are protected in a male-dominated world. Women generally fear social disapproval more than men and therefore tend to observe prevailing mores to a greater extent that do males. Walter Reckless in *The Crime Problem* (1961)[9] calls attention to some of the specifics which characterize female criminality. To think of the criminality of women in the same order of phenomena as crime in general is to cloud the issue. Theories which attempt to explain criminality in males fall short in explaining criminality in females, due to the biological make-up of women and, still more, because of the role women play in male-dominated societies. The woman must not only be herself, but also "play up to, for, or with men," the latter role giving her a "second self to an initial self."

Since the theories of Lombroso, Thomas, Pollak and Cohen were not supported by data collected to test an hypothesis, Barbara A. Kay (1961)[10] designed research to test specific hypothesis regarding components of the self-definition (concept) of females in Crime. In her unpublished Ph.D. dissertation, "Differential Self-Perceptions Among Female Offenders," she sought to explain the chief aspects of the female prisoner's self as she perceived it in the institution, to assess her direction of socialization, to measure the extent to which she perceived herself as being alienated and, finally, to approximate the way in which she perceived the institution was affecting her. Most of the 350 Ohio Reformatory for Women inmates assisted in this study. Dr. Kay's research reveals that the younger inmates (under 33 years old) were veering toward poor socialization much more frequently than older inmates (33 years old and over). Women who began delinquent careers before they were fourteen years old were more poorly socialized than those who started delinquency after fourteen. No significant socialization differences were found regarding the number of arrests or the length of incarceration. As to alienation, no important variations were found between inmates according to age, number of previous arrests, the length of time already spent in the institution and age at the initial onset of delinquency. However, Dr. Kay found that the alienation of the women inmates was not much more pronounced than that experienced by professional women, factory workers and shopgirls. This is conceptualized by Kay as "role lag."

Because of their role in a male-dominated society, according to Dr. Kay, women generally, including female offenders, feel more helpless in society than do men. "Role lag" refers to the discrepancy between what is conceded to be the equal position of women in the United States today and their actual status; women are categorically discriminated against as members of the "weaker sex," much as are other minority group members. The judicial process metes out differential sentencing for the female, and all this to the benefit of womankind if the price paid for the privileges is not considered. Today's woman has to wear a variety of hats. She must change roles frequently and the roles may lack consistency and continuity. If her control system is lacking or deficient, she will feel dissociated from society, powerless to control her destiny and hopeless as she drifts through uncontrollable situations. Heretofore, researchers have tried to understand the woman's concept of her being by observing her "looking-glass self"—beauty culture, the hairdo, a nice dress. Needed now, Dr. Kay holds, is an endeavor to reach the innerself perceived by oneself without a mirror.

This subordination of the feminine role in a male-dominated

society is not without some advantage. As Henry Clay Smith indicates in his *Personality Adjustment* (1961),[11] women are more sociable and warmer than men. But although these are qualities related to being a poor judge, women have more motivation for understanding others and are, therefore, likely to be better judges than men. The typical woman in our society finds that the attentions she receives depends less upon her objective accomplishments than upon her personal conquests. The ability to recognize subtle indications of favor, disfavor, rivalry and defeat are vital to her.

Among the more recent, significant contributions toward understanding the delinquent girl is the study by Leo J. Trese,[12] *101 Delinquent Girls* (1962). Father Trese, a parish priest of the Archdiocese of Detroit, served as a chaplain at a residential school for socially maladjusted girls conducted by the Sisters of the Good Shepherd. Among the number of his useful conclusions that may serve as guidelines to future research by other investigators are the following: (a) there is need to detect as early as possible in the life of the child, the signs of potential delinquent behavior, otherwise the task of modifying patterns of behavior becomes progressively more difficult and discouraging; (b) mere words are futile in changing delinquent behavior—a perceived love is the line over which the spoken words must travel; what is true of words is doubly true of punishment; (c) the girls, however they may vary from one another in their feelings towards adults, are, without exception, heavily loaded with negative feelings towards their mothers—all of them are greatly in need of a worthy mother figure with whom to identify. At one point in his study, Trese describes himself as their only "father image" during this particular time in their lives.

A case presentation of the delinquent trends and mechanism of a four-year-old girl, which demonstrates August Aichhorn's theory of the libidinal structure of the neurotic delinquent and characteristics of youthful delinquents, is summarized in a compilation of psychoanalytic studies, *Searchlights On Delinquency,* by Edith Sterba.[13] This four-year old delinquent syndrome was expressed in "her stealing bicycles, her running away, her attempts to seduce and undress other children, the sex play with little boys and taking their penises in her mouth, her continuous fighting with her siblings and other children, and her bedwetting." The author stated that because of the mother's extreme defensiveness it was impossible to determine exactly how much of this girl's delinquent behavior was manifested at the time she was referred. The child's symptoms did not assume the proportions found in juvenile delinquents because of her age, which made possible for her mother's complete restriction. The complete freedom of expression with which she acted out her symptoms in play, the irresistible ` urge and the unusual amount of material revealed, indicated clearly that had she been older she would have acted out these symptoms in reality. Case material revealed conflict and confusion about the role of the male and the female and insight into the structure of her libidinal development, especially in regard to the complex ramifications of the preoedipal mother fixation and the transition to a father fixation. Insight into the development of her superego was also revealed. Although this girl was treated successfully in unfavorable home conditions, the author concluded that the therapeutic results illustrate the value of analytically trained social workers and suggest the need for increasing the numbers trained in this field. She concludes, further, that it points to the need for institutions where young children with symptoms of incipient delinquency can be placed whenever the home environment makes treatment there impossible.

John C. Collidge, in a case presentation illustrates the psychodynamics of the delinquency of a fifteen-year-old girl whose behavior expressed underlying family pathology in an article entitled "Brother Identification in an Adolescent Girl".[14] The mother's vicarious gratification from this fifteen-year-old girl's delinquent behavior of stealing, truancy and lying was revealed. The neurotic interactions within the family group and her psychic disturbances are discussed. Her primitive ego defenses and the intensity and seriousness of her compulsive acting out were very striking in this presentation.

For deeper insights and a greater understanding of the delinquent girl, it is necessary to review some major aspects of the female role in American culture. It is important, also, to consider some basic psychological principles as they apply to women.

Florence Kluckhalm[15] states that in reviewing the history of the woman's role in the United States, it becomes evident that for many years a central issue has been her demand for the right to participate more fully in all those activities in which dominant American values are expressed. Because of the kind of education women of today receive, the issue has become more acute in recent years.

> Girls are no longer trained in markedly different ways or for different things than boys are. Throughout childhood and youth the girl goes to school with boys and is taught very much as they are taught. From babyhood on, she learns the ways of being independent and autonomous, and she is expected to know how to look after herself all through adolescence and beyond—forever if need be. The hope is expressed, of course, that she will not have to remain independent and will not therefore need to use much of what she has learned. Instead, and this is the truly great problem, she is expected upon her marriage, or certainly after the children are born, to give her attention to all those things which are defined as feminine and for which she has not been well trained at all.

The author concludes that "it is not to be wondered that the strains in the feminine role are numerous and make for serious personality difficulties in many women."

Robert Coughlin, in an article entitled, "Changing Roles in Modern Marriage," in *Life Magazine's* special issue on the American woman,[16] relates that the industrial revolution produced an unsettling effect on the emotional lives of both men and women, and women in particular. He states that many psychiatrists believe that the sudden change destroyed the traditional basis for women's self-respect—her confidence in her own value to society. Her home, the center of her deepest emotional satisfactions, lost not only its economic value but most of the educational and recreational aspects which she had supervised. In discussing the emotional needs of the female and the male and the general trends, he states that:

> Psychiatrists fear that the general trend of American society is unhealthy. Spottily and sporadically, but increasingly, the sexes in this country are losing their identities. The emerging American woman tends to be assertive and exploitive. The emerging American man tends to be passive and irresponsible.

Margaret Mead, in the same *Life* article, states that American women are not thought of as a weak and subservient sex:

> We think of men and women as being pretty much alike in their capabilities, in their interests, and in their roles. Much of the confusion that exists for women today is attributed to the striking paradox of women who are educated like men and who can do most of the things men do but who still are taught to prefer marriage to any other way of life. American women have come a long way on the road toward a role for women which is as dignified and responsible as the one assigned to men.[17]

Allison Davis and his collaborators elaborate, in their studies on the dominant value differences between lower and middle-class children and adults, white and black. In the lower-class pattern of life, a high premium is placed on free expression of aggression, on spending and sharing and on immediate physical gratification:

> Cleanliness, respect for property, sexual control, achievement are of lesser importance to the lower-class family than to the middle class. The middle-class is encouraged to work and pressured to work for relatively distant goals; his parents take for granted that he will achieve these goals, and the child, too, comes to take his ultimate goals for granted.[18]

In the lower class, L. L. LeShan describes the time orientation as one of:

> quick sequences of tension and relief. One does not frustrate oneself for long periods of plan action with goals far in the future. The future, generally, is an indefinite, vague, diffuse region and its rewards and punishments are too uncertain to have much motivating value. In this class, one errs when he is hungry.[19]

In describing certain aspects of life in the lower-class black family in Chicago during the depression and early years of World War II, Drake and Cayton state:

> Lower-class men are in a weak economic position vis-a-vis their women and children. Male control loosened, the woman becomes the dominant figure. Since she pays the piper, she usually feels justified in calling the tune. But while lower-class men are in a weak economic position, they are in a strategic position otherwise. Black lower-class women, like all women, have their affectional and sexual needs. Being predominantly working women of limited education, unable to spend time or money in

"prettifying" themselves, they cannot hope to get husbands from the middle class and upper class. They also face the sexual competition of the most attractive lower-class girls, who can get men to support them, and of the prostitutes and semi-prostitutes. In a sense, therefore, most lower-class women have to take love on male terms. The men, on the other hand, are strongly tempted to take advantage of such a situation and trade love for a living. The net result is an attitude of suspicion toward men blended with a woman's natural desire to be loved for herself alone.[20]

In a recent study under the guidance of Dr. Lois Pratt,[21] associate professor of sociology, students in classes in juvenile delinquency and criminology at Fairleigh Dickinson University, Rutherford, New Jersey, interviewed women involved in major categories of antisocial behavior. In the university's publication, an issue was devoted to the "Ills of Modern Women."

The writers considered the problems of alcoholism, drug addiction, larceny and murder. All are significant for the individual and for society, yet, as they state, they have not been "adequately researched as problems of women."

Although the gap is decreasing, there are fewer women than men who drink. Difficulty with such statistics lies in the fact that women alcoholics tend to remain hidden. They take great pains to conceal their drinking and alcohol. As drinking becomes more socially acceptable behavior for women and as women join ranks previously restricted to men, using "utilitarian" drinking for business and social reasons, a new group of women problem-drinkers may emerge.

Certain feminine qualities make most women less susceptible than men to addiction to narcotic drugs. Most female addicts are prostitutes. Many prostitutes turn to drugs to make their lives more bearable and, once addicted, are forced to remain prostitutes to support their habits. The authors observe that although both sexes have the same inherent impulses to enhance pleasure and relieve pain by artificial means, females, on the average, are more sensitive to the taboos of society and less likely to indulge in practices that are socially condemned. The fact that women appear to have respect for, as well as fear of, the law was evidenced, according to the writers, when there was a marked decline in the proportion of female addicts in 1915 when addiction became a federal crime with severe punishment for convicted offenders.

The fact that larceny has increased among female offenders is related to the social forces affecting women. Most forms of larceny involve little physical danger, force and daring. In crime, women tend to be influenced by society's rule that women should not engage in violence or should not be aggressive.

Shoplifting and petty theft from employers, by a household maid for example, are typical thefts for women. Teen-age girls constitute a significant number of the shoplifters and, as in other activities, they usually work in twos or threes acting as a clique. They concentrate generally on stealing accessories, small leather goods and clothing, according to a report by a New Jersey suburban store where 50 per cent of all the shoplifters arrested were teen-age girls. With the increasing use of coin-operated devices and self-service displays, the incidence of shoplifting has risen among women, who, in general, are the primary shoppers in our society.

In the case of murder, it is reported that motives of jealousy, frustration, humiliation and emotional sensitivity are frequently observed. The victims traditionally have been members of the murderer's family, usually husbands when the security of the woman within the home is threatened by a rival. The second most frequent type of homicide committed by the female is infanticide—the illegitimate child most frequently is the victim.

The authors of the Fairleigh Dickenson University study summarize the following points in particular:

1. Women are less likely than men to commit most types of crime and to indulge in most types of antisocial behavior.
2. When women do commit crimes or socially deviant acts, they are more likely than men to carry them out furtively and secretly, and also more likely to be protected from the consequences.
3. Social change is affecting both the incidence and the character of women's delinquency. Dr. Pratt elaborates:

In the main, women have derived enormous benefits from the social changes of recent decades. There has been a very real liberation from ignorance, drudgery and confinement. However, as women moved into the mainstream of community business, education and political life, they have come to experience the frustration, aggravations and abrasions that were formerly absorbed by men.[22]

Additional insights have been made available to those interested in the plight of delinquent girls, especially the female institutionalized delinquent, in the publication of *Institutional Rehabilitation Of Delinquent Youth* by the National Conference of Superintendents of Training Schools and Reformatories.[23] The raw material of this volume was actually in preparation over a period of thirty-five years. Twenty-eight superintendents and other specialists were invited to submit drafts of chapters on many subjects. These were then edited by Superintendent Donald D. Scarborough, New York State Vocational Institution, West Coxsackie, New York, and Superintendent Abraham G. Novick, New York State Training School for Girls, Hudson, New York. In a chapter entitled, "The Female Institutionalized Delinquent," Novick makes some comparisons regarding the expression of delinquency by males and females:

> Male delinquency is largely expressed in aggressive acting-out activities, such as stealing, robbery, assault and breaking and entering. Female delinquency is largely sexual delinquency, running away from home and truancy. The male offender, thus, tends to hurt others, while the female hurts herself. This dichotomy in self-expression along sexual lines permeates human activity at all age levels. The differences are largely due to the role expectations of the boy and girl in our society as well as to basic variations in the psychosexual development of male and female.

Reference is made to the fact that literature regarding female delinquency has been primarily limited to concern about the social consequences. Etiology, or differentiating female from male delinquency, has been treated with comparative indifference in research literature. The tendency has been to write about offenders in terms of the male, and how females may be influenced by the quantity and quality of male delinquency and the attention and interest drawn to this area by society.

In order to understand fully the significance of the female individual or group behavior in an institutional setting, Novick summarized that cultural expectations and, in part, physical structure tend to:

> (a) foster a dependency role for the female, with life goal achieved through marriage and family and strong needs to be loved, accepted and protected; (b) develop social techniques in order for the female to cope with her male environment; (c) place considerable emphasis on narcissistic attributes for making oneself attractive to the male; (d) permit open expression of affection toward members of the same sex.[24]

In institutions, the female counterpart of the male informal group is the make-believe family, which is peculiarly suited to meeting ingrained dependency needs and temporary aspirations of delinquent girls. Punishment only intensified and solidifies its anti-staff function. A more positive approach stresses group incentives for the make-believe family, utilizing it as a treatment force in changing delinquent values. The outstanding value of this study is the fact that the information comes from those "on the firing line," from those closest to the problems under consideration.

In her study of several hundred adolescent delinquent girls (13 to 19 years of age) in institutions in Minnesota, Gisela Konopka[25] concluded that these girls had in common fear and distrust of adults and authority figures, poor self-images, a deep sense of isolation, and lack of communication with others. Four key concepts that she proposed as basic to these common problems are as follows:

1. The unique dramatic biological onset of puberty for which these girls are unprepared. Although some adolescent girls in the middle socioeconomic class communicate among themselves and sometimes with adults about the facts and meaning of these biological changes, girls in the lower socioeconomic group have less communication with both peers and adults and often associate puberty with physical injury and other fear-generating events. The task of bearing children influences the girls' total attitudes toward sex. The experience of pregnancy appears to change the girl but generally there is an attitude of, "let's get it over with fast."

2. Complex identity problems differ from those of boys in intensity and scope in the traditional way, but are aggravated for girls in low-income families by the inferior, undesirable status of the women they know and the frequent absence of a father in the home or his brutal treatment of his wife. While

some girls are helped to understand and make positive use of the process of separating from their mothers by establishing an early love relationship with the father, many girls have no such help and this influences their attitudes toward both sexes for the rest of their lives. This becomes a strong factor in the girls' attachment to peers, male or female. Some girls remained attached to other girls because they had never been able to move into a heterosexual relationship. This was due to fear of men because of their fathers' treatment of the girls' mothers or inability to compete with other girls for the attention and affection of young men because they had so little self-confidence and harbored low estimates of their self-worth. Another factor affecting the amount of homosexuality among the girls Dr. Konopka studied was the comparative safety of a homosexual relationship, which could not produce an unwanted child.

3. Rapidly changing cultural patterns give today's adolescent girls no tradition of preparation for vocational roles, including those of wife and mother. Emancipation of women was stepped up during and after the second World War but society has not yet fully accepted this change. The adult world of the United States is still highly conflicted about the position of women in it. For instance, while the girl is educated to choose her place in the working life of the community and is encouraged to become a participating citizen, she finds frequent job discrimination and is often urged to reject her intellect. All of this produces value conflicts of an extremely intense nature at the time when adolescent girls are forced to deal with many other value conflicts that are expected in the maturation process.

4. A faceless adult authority seemed to prevail in the lives of these girls. They exhibited little confidence in adults. Most of them could not name one adult with whom they could relate and in whom they had confidence and trust. An unwed mother spoke with surprise about her ease in talking with her parents. Others said they found they could talk with parents only after they were in trouble. Help in handling authority was alien to most of the girls in the study and they resented it. The girls did not blame their parents, but rather saw their parents as part of the adult world which was strange and hostile to them. The most frequent and telling criticism the girls had of adults concerned adult hypocrisy.

Edgar W. Butler, describes an empirical classification system which was based upon an analysis of a California delinquent-girl population . . . the Las Palmas School for Girls.[26] He employed a sample of 139 subjects selected as representative of all girls who were ever placed in this institution. At intake each girl filled out a Jesness Psychological Inventory of 155 items concerning attitudes towards such diverse factors as family, school, police and "self." In summary, the three major types derived from this analysis were as follows: Type I—disturbed-neurotic, Type II—immature-impulsive and Type III—covert manipulators. The descriptions of girls in each type were accomplished by evaluating differentiating items and by the operational staff's perceptions of the three groups of girls.

Type I (disturbed-neurotic) appears to be concerned with procedures, regularity, order and law and a readiness to accept cultural norms. Over-internalization of rules and standards may be involved. Self-control and ritualism are primary dimensions, but these have been put aside by delinquent acts and there is evidence of guilt feelings and neurotic reactions. Independent evaluations by staff members of the institution include such descriptions as passive-withdrawn, anxious, depressive and conformer. One operational staff member states that the Type I girl appears to be those who have become delinquent as a result of some interpersonal situation with which they cannot cope and they react through delinquent behavior. The delinquency pattern in this type is seen as being of relatively recent origin and presumably of short duration.

With the Type II (immature-impulsive) there is a rejection of ritualistic behavior and external controls. Immediate gratification is of primary importance and impulsive behavior results in punitive sanctions. Behavior patterns appear to reflect manifest attitudes. Immaturity, impulsiveness, and lack of internal integration and control is the emerging picture in this group. These girls rebel against authority. Evaluations by staff members include descriptions of aggressiveness, impulsiveness and overt manipulation, with evidence of immaturity and sociopathic tendencies.

Butler found that girls in Type III (convert manipulators) are self-assertive and attempt to control their environment. They are ritualistic and are overly concerned with external appearances and reputation. Overt behavior is oriented toward the expected, but latent attitudes are at variance with behavior. Conforming behavior is observed as long as expectations and structures are given. However, covert manipulation is continuous. These girls are described by the institutional staff as clever, intelligent manipulators, with sociopathic and aggressive tendencies. When first institutionalized, these girls are "hidden" or covert manipulators. Once their manipulative activities are discovered and countermeasures taken, these girls become aggressive, snarling and hostile. This type of girl proves to be the most provocative. She falsified the test and gives expected answers—responses that do not reflect her attitudes, but responses that make her appear "good." The author stated that this girl can confuse an institutional staff with a farce that may take months to penetrate.

In utilizing this study for classification purposes one must recognize that the subcultural or gang type does not appear. The author explains that this type was not included in this research because of her systematic exclusion from the institution where the research was conducted.

The value of this research project is that it has resulted in an objective general typological system that has relevance for selecting kinds of supervisors and has utility for assigning delinquents to alternative treatment modalities.[27]

The Children's Bureau reports that delinquency among girls is rising sixteen times faster than among boys throughout the nation, although the teen population has risen only 2.4 per cent. In large metropolitan juvenile courts, in order of frequency, girls were referred for running away, ungovernable behavior, larceny and sex offenses. Running away and ungovernable behavior are often related offenses, and these together with various types of sex offenses comprise almost half of all girls' delinquency cases handled by the courts.

In countries where, by tradition, women are kept to a purely domestic role, playing no part in the social and economic sectors, their crime rate is correspondingly low. As women become emancipated, so the proportion of women among convicted persons increases.

Ruth Morris in her study in Flint, Michigan, compared matching groups of delinquent and nondelinquent boys and girls.[28] To a significant extent, the delinquent girls have the highest incidence of broken homes or homes beset by quarrels and tensions. They are more often untidy and neglected in personal appearance. She found that male delinquents often appear to be boisterous, exuberant boys who find satisfaction among their rebellious peers. Girls do not receive the same support from the delinquent subculture as the boys, although they are admitted on the fringes of male gangs.

Another difference appears at puberty. Morris states that the wayward boy usually engages in stealing and breaking-in and only occasionally a sex offender; the wayward girl more often takes to sexual misconduct. This behavior serves as an effective upsetting form of protest against the attitudes and restrictions of older relatives. Often it appears to be a way of searching for the affection which was wanting in an unhappy parental home.

All young girls who run away from unhappy homes into the arms of a lover should not be considered promiscuous. Some of them form emotional attachments as strong as they are unsuitable.

Elizabeth O'Kelly, in a study of girls in an English school, contrasted the background of thieves and sexual delinquents. She found that while both groups come mostly from disturbed homes, the thieves frequently suffer separation from or rejection by parents, while the sexual delinquent more often has difficult relations with fathers and mothers who are conjugally unstable.[29] There is a perennial problem of "situational homosexuality" (honey business) in training schools for girls.[30]

REFERENCES

1. Lombroso, Caesar, and Ferrero, William: *The Female Offender.* York and London, Appleton, 1916, pp. 109-111.
2. Fernald, Mabel Ruth, *et al.*: *A Study of Women Delinquents in New York State.* New York, Century, 1920, p. 525.
3. Thomas, William I.: *The Unadjusted Girl.* Boston, Little, 1923, pp. 1-69.
4. Glueck, Sheldon, and Eleanor T.: *Five Hundred Delinquent Women.* New York, Knopf, 1934, p. 288.

5. Kemp, Tage: Physical and Psychological Causes of Prostitution. Geneva, League of Nations Advisory Committee on Social Questions, No. 26, May 28, 1943, p. 53.

6. Pollak, Otto: *The Criminality of Women.* Philadelphia, U of Pa Pr, 1950, pp. 1-7.

7. Cohen, Albert K.: *Delinquent Boys: The Culture of the Gang.* Glencoe, Free Pr, 1955, p. 45.

8. Barnes, Narry Elmer, and Tetters, Negley K.: *New Horizons in Criminology.* New York, P-H, 1959, pp. 61-64.

9. Reckless, Walter: *The Crime Problem.* New York, Appleton, 1967, pp. 98ff, 148ff.

10. Kay, Barbara A.: Differential Self Perceptions Among Female Offenders. Unpublished Ph.D. thesis, Ohio State University, 1961.

11. Smith, Henry Clay: *Personality Adjustment.* New York, McGraw, 1961, p. 68.

12. Trese, Leo J.: *101 Delinquent Girls.* Notre Dame, Fides, 1962, p. 77.

13. Eissler, K. R.: *Searchlights on Delinquency.* New York, Int Univs, 1956, pp. 102-114.

14. Collidge, John C.: Brother identification in an adolescent girl. *Am J Orthopsychiatry, XXIV* (No. 3):611-645, July 1954.

15. Kluckhalm, Florence: In Kluckhohn, Clyde, Murray, Henry A., and Schneider, David M. (eds): *Personality in Nature, Society and Culture.* New York, Knopf, 1953, pp. 356,364.

16. Coughlin, Robert: Changing roles in modern marriage. *Life, 41* (No. 26): 109-118, December 24, 1956.

17. Mead, Margaret: Ibid., pp. 26-27.

18. Davis, Allison, *et al*: Quoted In Leightton, Alexander H., Clausen, John A., and Wilson, Robert H. (eds): *Explorations in Social Psychiatry.* New York, Basic Books, 1957, p. 258.

19. LeShan, L. L.: Time orientation and social class. *J Abnorm Soc Psychol,* p. 589, 1947.

20. Drake, St. Clair, and Cayton, Horace R.: *Black Metropolis.* New York, Harcourt, 1945, pp. 583-584.

21. Pratt, Lois: Women in trouble. *This Week Magazine,* Chicago Daily News, July 31, 1965, p. 5.

22. Ibid., p. 12.

23. Novick, Abraham G.: The female institutionalized delinquent. In *Institutional Rehabilitation of Delinquent Youth.* Albany, Delmar, 1962, p. 158.

24. Ibid., p. 160.

25. Konopka, Gisela: *The Adolescent Girl in Conflict.* Englewood Cliffs, P-H, 1966, pp. 120-28.

26. Butler, Edgar W.: Personality Dimensions of Delinquent Girls. *Criminologica, 3* (No. 1): 7-10, May 1965.
27. Bloch, Herbert A., and Flynn, Frank T.: *Delinquency: The Juvenile Offender in America Today.* New York, Random, 1956, pp. 198-202.
28. Morris, Ruth R.: Female delinquencies and relational problems. *Social Forces, 43*:82-89, 1964.
29. O'Kelly, Elizabeth: Delinquent girls and their parents. *Br J Educ Psychol, 28*:59-66, 1955.
30. Vedder, Clyde B., and King, Patricia G.: *Problems of Homosexuality in Corrections.* Springfield, Thomas, 1967.

CHAPTER 4

THE RUNAWAY GIRL

SINCE RUNNING AWAY FROM HOME is one of the most common forms of acting-out in the adolescent girl, it was expected that runaway behavior would result in the highest percentage of commitments reported by the training school for girls.

The pathogenic elements involved in runaway behavior of girls have received limited attention in psychiatric literature. The importance of the unresolved oedipal conflict in the etiology of running away in boys was first postulated by Rosenheim in 1940.[1] Since then, other studies have shown that the oedipal conflict and the threat of an incestuous relationship also are important causative factors of running away.

In a study made in a court clinic which serves an essentially middle-class suburban population, Robey, Rosenwald, Snell and Lee found that of the entire caseload of 293 adolescent girls brought before the court during a ten-year period, 162 (55%) were runaways. The girls' age ranged from thirteen to seventeen years and six months, the main age being fifteen years and three months. This study excluded those who had not stayed away overnight and those who denied the intent to run away.

They emphasized that running away, hardly a childish escapade, is generally indicative of some severe individual or family pathology and may result from a wide variety of intolerable home situations. The cause most frequently observed in their study was the unconscious threat of an incestuous relationship with the father, the fear of the resultant dissolution of the family and the concurrent depression.[2]

Basic to the etiology of running away was a consistent pattern of family interaction: a disturbed marital relationship, inadequate control by the parents over their own impulses, and the girl's deprivation of love of the mother and subtle pressure by her to have the daughter assume the maternal role.

Prior to the onset of adolescence, this role can be assumed in most cases. However, with the breakdown of the prepubescent defenses, the girl acquires an increasingly bitter attitude of rebellion in her role and finally runs away.

The authors of this study contend that the act of running away, a legal form of juvenile delinquency, is often treated lightly by the parents, the police and the courts unless it becomes chronic or appears in conjunction with sexual acting-out or related delinquent behavior. They conclude that running away is the result of a complex neurotic interaction between the parents and the daughter in a "triangle" situation. Its seriousness as a symptom calls for far greater concern than is presently given by most parents and law enforcement officials.[3]

Several studies have probed the backgrounds of high school students, socially accepted and playing the role of nondelinquents. In one study, high school and correctional school students were compared as to the frequency and seriousness of delinquent acts, including running from home. Questionnaires were anonymously completed by high school students in three small western communities and by inmates in a western training school for female delinquents. A much higher percentage of the training school girls checked offenses. The comparison of high school and training school youth is significant for repeated offenses. In their study on reported delinquent behavior among girls in high school and correctional school, James F. Short, Jr. and F. Ivan Nye revealed that 11.3 per cent of the high school girls admitted running away from home, while 85.5 per cent of the correctional school girl admitted running away from home more than once or twice, while 51.8 per cent of the correctional school girls admitted running away from home more than twice.[4]

In a more detailed analysis, the authors indicated that in their sample of students, a small percentage of boys and girls exceeded the training school groups in delinquency, but in general, the boys and girls sent to the training school were more persistently and seriously delinquent than the high school students.

It is typical of girls not to assume a delinquent manner of behavior as often as boys. Nevertheless, 30 per cent or more of the high school girls had driven a car without a driver's license, skipped school, or defied parental authority. They have taken little things worth less than two dollars and bought or drunk beer or wine, including drinking at home.

As indicated by Short and Nye, there is considerable female delinquency that is never revealed, including running away from home. For the most part, juvenile delinquency becomes hidden delinquency—as true today as in yesteryear. A Boston study revealed that in 1946, of some 6,416 infractions of the law by juveniles, only 91 were brought to official action. Over six hundred of these infractions were considered serious, but only sixty-eight of the perpetrators were prosecuted.[5]

Running away is the principal offense leading to the commitment of girls. The following pages of this chapter contain four actual case histories of runaway girls with identifiable material omitted.

Delores R.

Delores R., a girl from a large metropolitan area, was 15 years, 10 months of age when she was committed to a girls' training school by a juvenile court because of chronic runaway behavior. The immediate circumstance leading to her commitment was her absence from home for several days.

At the training school Delores was described as a dependent, rejected girl who not only felt inadequate, but lacked insight into her behavior. She felt rejected by her mother and their relationship was inadequate in meeting Delores' needs. The lack of a consistent father figure, as well as her limited intellectual functioning all contributed to her feelings of confusion and defeat. Initially, Delores attempted to handle her feelings by psychological withdrawal; this having failed, she acted-out by leaving home. She had been subjected to pressure beyond her capacity.

Her mother was described as intelligent and apparently interested in her daughter and her future welfare. However, she failed to recognize Delores' limitations.

During her placement at the training school, Delores was happy in a relaxed program. Consistent with her level of academic achievement, she was placed at the fourth-grade level. Her teachers found her very pleasant and cooperative. She became comfortable in adult relationships and more sociable. She rejected returning home and expressed a strong desire to live with a maternal aunt and her husband who resided near the home of her grandparents. The mother was willing to accept this plan and Delores made a satisfactory adjustment in this home during her entire parole period.

Apparently, Delores' unfortunate choice of runaway behavior was the result of extreme stress since she was unable to gain approval (deeply needed). In addition to delinquency needs, she lacked the intellectual capacity to learn social skills necessary for positive interaction with her peers. Consequently, she was unable to gratify her needs outside the home or in school. The prolonged frustration of these needs undoubtedly precipitated her immature attempt to gain release through avoidance (running away to escape the stress). Fortunately, placement with an approving aunt who attempted to help meet her needs enabled her to learn more appropriate ways of behaving.

Susan R.

Susan is a white girl, 16 years, 10 months old, from a small urban community who was committed because of runaway behavior and drunkenness. Court information disclosed that Susan had been involved in several delinquent acts. Her behavior consisted of running away, drinking and sexual delinquency with older men. At the time of her admission to the training school, Susan freely expressed that many family arguments and general unhappy home conditions precipitated her running away as a means of escape. One year prior to her commitment to the training school, she was admitted to a state hospital for excessive drinking. She received an unconditional release two months after admittance.

Susan, the eighth of eleven children, was reared in a chaotic and deprived family setting. The three youngest children lived at home while the others were either married or had moved away from the family. There was much overt hostility between Susan and two older sisters. Susan attributed their leaving home and premarital pregnancies to the unpleasant home conditions.

Susan's mother was described as a very unkempt person maintaining a very undesirable home. Family income came primarily from the father's seasonal employment and unemployment compensation. Susan began school at the age of six years and attended the same school until she completed the eighth grade. She completed one year of high school and interacted well with the faculty members and her peers while in school. She had several part-time jobs working as a waitress in various delicatessens. She was unable to keep jobs very long because of the tendency to lose her temper and quit.

The staff at the training school diagnosed Susan as having suffered extreme frustration in the home setting, especially in the area of dependency needs. She was ambivalent toward her mother and had a strong need to seek attention and identification with an accepting adult. She described her mother as inadequate and unable to provide emotional support for Susan and her feelings. She expressed much hostility toward the father.

Susan utilized several different types of behavior to offset her frustration in the home setting. Her original attempts were along socially acceptable lines i.e. school performance and part-time jobs to gain approval. However, her deep-seated frustration and unmet needs interfered with her acquiring the necessary emotional controls to adhere to these avenues for an extended period. She also had only models of immature anger and hostility in her home and, therefore, responded to frustration in like manner.

While at the training school, Susan expressed a desire to live in a foster home after her release from the school. She had gained sufficient insight to realize that she would never be able to make an acceptable parole adjustment in her own home. She later was paroled to the home of a couple in a nearby community who had taken an interest in her. Because of her inability to cope with her home situation, she left home and turned to alcohol as a psychological escape. However, because one's depression and feelings of rejection are intensified under the influence of alcohol, Susan engaged in promiscuous activities to enhance her feelings of worth and desirability.

Alicia A.

Alicia A. is a fifteen year old white girl who was committed by Family Court because of runaway behavior and truancy. On two occasions she was absent from her home for two-day periods. These were handled by the police, who released her to her parents with a warning. At the time of commitment she had run away for two-week periods on three different occasions, twice living in an apartment with other girls and once working as a baby-sitter for a woman she had met casually. In each case she said she did not want to return to school and did not want to go home lest she be whipped.

Alicia is the second of five children. There is an older sister, a younger sister and two younger brothers. She is the only one who has caused any trouble. She is easily led by friends who have delinquent histories. Although her father has never had any formal education, he owns a small neighborhood business. The mother, an elementary school graduate, works in a factory to assist financially. The father's business requires him to remain open evenings while the mother works a late afternoon and evening shift. The parents maintain a very nice apartment in an area which has a high crime rate among adults and children.

The family relationship was relatively good at the time of her commitment, although formerly the parents were separated for several years. The mother seemed to accept Alicia as generally docile and immature and blamed Alicia's girl friend for leading her into delinquency. The mother considered Alicia as the father's favorite child and said, "Alicia knows that she is much loved at home." The father, however, was quite strict and used corporal punishment. Both parents have a language handicap which, together with their lack of knowledge of American customs, tends to interfere with their understanding of their daughter's general adjustment problems. The mother stated that the father was very lonely for Alicia. She indicated resentment of her daughter's relationship with her husband.

Alicia was described as an impulsive, attractive, well-developed girl who enjoyed dancing, sports and cooking. She was very sociable and preferred to associate with older boys and girls. She was a girl of average intellectual ability, but made very poor school progress. She was greatly retarded in reading while in the school in the community. She was transferred to a special school because of truancy and behavior difficulties. At the training school she was given remedial reading and placed in a half-day school program. She progressed rapidly and soon requested a full school program where she continued to advance to her proper grade placement and made a good adjustment.

Although Alicia's mother did not reject her openly, she considered her immature and docile. This silent disapproval hardly helped Alicia's self-esteem and when she could not gain the level of acceptance she needed in the home, she sought the approval of other authority figures, e.g. her teachers. Unfortunately, her lack of success in school reinforced her feelings of unworthiness. She felt unaccepted by her parents, teachers and schoolmates. She then turned to other peers for approval and followed their suggestions although her parents disapproved. To avoid failure in school, she began to run away. The more she ran away the poorer she did in school and the lower she fell in the estimation of those whom she originally sought to please. As an intense dislike for school developed, she stayed away from home for extended periods of time, fearing the punishment and further rejection upon returning.

Once Alicia was able to experience success and find support and approval from the staff, she began to value herself. Furthermore, she developed the controls necessary to adhere to a full school schedule successfully.

Both Delores and Alicia sought to escape the stress and anxiety associated with failure. Unable to find enough acceptance to satisfy their dependency needs, they ran away so as to avoid further frustration. Placement in the training school enabled them to gain a realistic appraisal of their potential and the skills and expectations in keeping with it. They were forced to cease running away and to cope with their problems.

Sally J.

Sally narrates her own story:

In Chicago, Illinois, at the . . . . Hospital, on the 27th day of December in the year 1948, at 10:30 p.m. an eight-and-a-half pound baby girl was born. The parents were young, the mother eighteen and the father twenty-two. The baby was named Sally. By now you have guessed this baby is I.

As a baby I spent a lot of time in the hospital. I was born with an extra finger and had trouble breathing through my nose. The finger had to be removed but they never did anything about my breathing.

At three months I was taken into the hospital with pneumonia I was finally released only to return with an alergy a few weeks later. I didn't have to stay long this time.

My paternal grandmother and great-grandmother lived on the second floor of our house. As far as I can remember I spent most of my time upstairs with them. It was a comfortable two story house. There was always a surprise or a treat for me upstairs. Sometimes I would try to help clean up, but at two years old I wasn't too good.

My maternal grandmother was then living in the Ida B. Wells Homes. I went to see her often. She has always been good with her hands. There was always a quilt to be made or something of that sort. Though I remember my maternal great-grandmother, I don't remember her name. Everyone called her "Mamma." Mamma was always baking cakes or cookies. Her cookies were known all over the neighborhood. Everybody loved mamma. She died in June, 1957 when I was eight years old.

In August, 1951 my parents were granted a divorce. I stayed with my grandmother until I was three and my mother remarried. My stepfather's name was Edward. This marriage was also short. While they were married we lived in Illinois, Missouri, Oregon and Michigan. They were separated after six months of marriage. He is now in New York. I never really liked him because he was always trying to make me do unpleasant things. Once he made me drink some buttermilk. I didn't like it so it wouldn't stay on my stomach and he gave me a whipping. When my mother finally found out what was going on she filed for a divorce.

My father is also remarried. His second marriage also lasted only a short time. Neither my father or my mother have ever had any more children. One reason is that my father, who was a professional boxer then, was hurt in the ring and was unable to reproduce any longer. My mother said she just didn't want anymore.

I was then moved again. My mother and I were living with my aunt, and her husband. They had six children of their own. While living there I attended Smith Branch Nursery School.

From there I went to my godmother for a year—then right back to my mother. I attended Louis Champion School for one semester. They gave me a double from kindergarten to first grade.

My godmother and her husband took me after this. They have a son a year and a half older than I. I attended Charles S. Deneen School from 1954 to 1961. I received two doubles, one from first to second grade and one from third to fourth grade. I then transferred to Parker Elementary School.

While attending Parker in 1961 I was living with my aunt and her husband and their three children. In Parker I received another double from seventh to eighth grade. My aunt saw me through grammer school and part of high school. I graduated from grammer school with honors in January, 1962. I had an I.Q of 114 and my reading was 10.7. The highest was math which was 11.3 plus— plus because 11.3 was as high as you could get on the test.

In January, 1963 my father was married again to Mary. She has three children, aged eighteen, seventeen and twelve.

In March, 1963 I moved in with my mother. By June I could see that my mother and I were not going to get along. It was neither all my fault nor all hers. So I started running away. By December, 1964 I had fifteen runaways, which is really nothing to be proud of.

During this time I was moved back and forth between my parents by the family court. January 5, 1965 they sent me to Geneva. Here I finally learned that running away from my problems did not prevent them. It is better to stay and face them. I left Geneva April 4, 1965 happy and some what relieved.

I went home to finish my education and live with my father and stepmother. I am now a senior in high school, although I am back in Geneva.

My father and Mary are still together. We now live in a twelve room house. My two stepbrothers and I will all graduate from high school this summer. My stepsister will come out of grammar school next year.

I returned to Geneva January 14, 1966 for pregnancy. I have plans to be married in November, 1966 if permission is granted by the parole board. The baby is due either the last of March or the first of April. I should be leaving some time in April. I hope the baby is a big healthy girl. Wish me luck!

When one reads this girl's account of her life, it becomes apparent that she has experienced relatively little security with her parents, even in early childhood. The traumatic illness, as an infant, caused prolonged separation which could have interfered with the development of love and deep trust in her mother. Furthermore, the marriage of her parents was dissolved before she was three so she had little remembrance of a stable family relationship. In fact, her only recollection of happiness and security seems to have been father's grandmother, who cared for her with much love and attention.

Starting with the divorce, she began a childhood of constant shuffling from one relative to another. Consequently, she had little opportunity to learn to love and respect her parents as responsible, capable persons who understood and cared for her. Instead, she was only aware of their failures in marriage.

During her elementary school years, Sally was fortunate in being in the homes of relatives who had fairly stable family relationship, i.e. two parents in the home. Apparently she felt that these persons were supportive, as she performed quite well academically and did not get into any difficulties.

However, as she entered early adolescence she was returned to live with her mother. At that age children need not only support and understanding, but structure and guidance as well, because their insecurities are increased by the many conflicts which arise during this period. The physical changes alone initiate fears and conflicts in relation to their sex role, social expectations (i.e. boy-girl relationships) and self-concept. Futhermore, there occurs a shift from utilizing parents and adults as models, to emulating peers, and confusion over appropriate behavior is further intensified by the normal stage of rebellion which accompanies this phase of their life. Consequently. unless the adolescent views his parents as consistent, stable and capable, he often rejects their values because they do not seem to have served the parents particularly well.

In Sally's case, it appears that neither parent was able to offer the love and structure which she needed and she began to run away to avoid dealing with her problems. It was not until she was confined in the training school that she began to realize the uselessness of that approach to life.

Unfortunately, once released from her structural environment, she again faced the conflicts and, still lacking the internal controls to deal with these, she once more got into trouble. It appears that her background of insecurity has greatly impeded her emotional development, so that she has been unable to adopt socially acceptable patterns of behavior through which she could realize her full potential.

Helen W.

It all started when I was 12 years old, just before my 13th birthday. And my father taught me how to drive. So I just started stealing the car all the time at the night times. My little brother was 9 years old at the time. He woke me up one night and indicated that he had seen me take off with the car one time and that he wanted me to take it again but take him for a ride this time. So we did. Then when we got away from the house he wanted to drive too, which he was to short to see over the sterring wheel. So I let him sit on my lap. We started driving around town for a couple of hours and then someone looked as if to me that they were following us. So we pulled into Par in Illinois. Right up the street from our house. When we were going around the corner of

the park I was looking out the rear view of my mirror and turned
the wrong way and I ran into a tree. All I can remember from
there is my brothers scream! And a lady came to the car and took
me up to the gulf course to put a cold towel on my mouth so it
would stop bleeding I had four stitches in my lip and lost my
front right tooth. My brother was rushed in an ambulance to coply
hospital. He was unconsious for at least 3 months. So I was placed
in my grandmothers house till things got settled down. Then
about 1 week later someone called her and she started crying over
the phone and rushed out of the house and said you stay here
with aunt and I'll be right back. Then my aunt told me that my
brother had died. For some odd reason I couldn't cry at the time.
When we went to the funeral. I tried to take my brother out of his
coffin and hold him for the last time. But everyone grabbed me
and made me sit down and tried to talk to me to make me settle
down. After I thought about what I did I felt as if I was just
going crazy at the time, and ever since he died for some reason
or another I just wanted to hurt myself or get hurt from some one
else. I guess that's only because I still feel guilty about the whole
thing and I feel as though it's all my fault. And no matter what
anyone tells me or how they try to put it in different word I'll
always feel the same pain and guilt inside of me. I just keep
wishing that it could of been me instead of him. So my father
use to put the blame all on me too all the time. He would just keep
throwing it up in my face. So I kept running away from home and
I finally got sent to retention homes and relations of mine and
to a group home and finally to a foster home. I never made it in
any of these places. I want to be back with my family and try to
make it at home once more. but I got sent to I.S.T.S.G. I've went
through a lot but now I'm ready to face reality and cope with my
problems that keep coming to me.

Isobel G.

My name is Isobel G. I am in here because, I ran away from
home so many times, Plus I could no stand my real mother or
step-father. Plus me and my cus had ran up this telephone bill
my cahanging it to other peoples number So then they found out
who was doing it and the manager of the telephone Company

came to my house, and asked alot of question, I came in May 4, And hope to be going home soon. My first time here. And going to try by best to make it my last time here. And I plan on doing that by working every day and any thing else to keep me out of here. 'I' think I did real goodfor myself while I been in here.It really helped me out alot,more then,I really was thinking it would do. So I better end this letter. By saying it was nice of you to think of use, by letteing of do this.

Catherine B.

My reason for being here is because Im a run away. I have ran away many times and was given many chances to change my ways. But kept on running away So the law sent me to Geneva January 24 1973 sence Ive been here I have learned many things about my self and other people I am also doing a lot of things for my self One is Ive gotten my drivers licenses and I am now in Nurses Aide. So when I do get out I will have a good training As for the people here they try there hardest to get you outta here AS for the girls there easy to live if you know how some think the rules are to live by but I think the rules are very good and if you do right you won't get in so much trouble And the staff will talk to you if you have a problem And they will do as much as they can to help you solve it I think the programs they have here are very good and Educational for us students like Nurses Aide and IBM and GED I guess all I really can say is that Geneva is what you make it.

Jane M.

The trouble all started when I was 13 yrs. old. I had just moved into Ill. I was in trouble 2 weeks after I got there. I ran away several times. Was put in House of Good Shepards and ran from there. Got caught 1 month later and stayed in detention 2 months, then I was sent to Geneva. Got paroled was out for 4 months and came back for curfew and trauncy. Have been here 5 months so far. I was locked up the first time February 17, 1972. Then I ran away March 28, 1972. The reason I was locked up for runaway. The probation officer said I was locked up for my own good and to get me off the street.

Conclusion

Numerous conditions seem to be involved as precipitating factors in these cases; early traumatic experiences, inadequate homes, parental rejection, sibling rivalry, unrealistic parental expectations, unstable marriages and inadequate communication between parents and children. In each case, however, the lack of satisfying experiences produced such frustration that the girl chose the immature defense of avoidance in trying to cope with her unmet needs. While this avenue of escape is least harmful to anyone but the girl herself, it usually serves little purpose, as the basic difficulties are not resolved.

REFERENCES

1. Rosenheim, F.: Techniques of therapy. *Am J Orthopsychiat*, p. 651, 1940.
2. Ames, Robey, Rosenwald, Richard J., Snell, John E., and Lee, Rita E.: The runaway girl: A reaction to family stress. *Am J Orthopsychiatry*, XXXIV:762-767, July, 1954.
3. Ibid, p. 765.
4. Short, James F., and Nye, F. Ivan: Extent of unrecorded juvenile delinquency tentative conclusions. *J Criminal Law, Criminology and Police Science, 49*:296-309, Nov-Dec, 1958.
5. Murphy, Fred J., Shirley, Mary M., and Witmer, Helen L.: The incidence of hidden delinquency. *Am J Orthopsychiatry, 16*: 686-696, 1946.

CHAPTER 5

THE INCORRIGIBLE GIRL

WHAT IS THE EXACT MEANING of "incorrigibility"? There is no consensus regarding this term. It can mean many things to many people, much as does the interpretation of "incompatibility" when used as grounds for divorce. As a term "Incompatibility" may mean "ungovernability," "uncontrollability," "beyond control of parents," "being obstinate" and/or "defying parental authority." As an illustration of judicial latitude and penal sanction in terms involving moral judgment, one offender, a sixteen-year-old boy, received a five year prison term from the judge of an adult criminal court. The Jacksonville (Fla.) *Time-Union* reported on February 5, 1952, that this was the first case tried under the new Florida Court Act, which permits the judge to send to adult criminal juveniles whom the judge considers "obstinate."

Many "incorrigible" girls are not brought to justice. In the study by Short and Nye referred to previously, 30.6 per cent of the high school girls had defied parental authority, while 68.3 per cent of the correctional school girls had defied parental authority. Continuation of this pattern was revealed in the fact that 5 per cent of the high school girls had defied their parents more than once or twice, but 39 per cent of the correctional school girls had defied their parents more than once or twice. Despite parental admonitions to the contrary, 58.2 per cent of the high school girls had driven a car without a driver's license or permit, and 68.3 per cent of the correctional school girls had done likewise. Recidivistic tendencies were noted in this study, as 29.9 per cent of the high school girls had driven cars without lawful permits more than once or twice, while 54.4 per cent of the correctional school girls also had driven cars without lawful permits more than once or twice.

✓ Incorrigibility strongly suggests a family disorganization symptom. Mabel Elliott believes that the virtues of honesty, faith and trust form the web, woof and pattern of responsible family life," quite important to the average woman; hence, lower female crime rates reflect a social situation pushing, to a greater degree, the males rather than the females toward crime.[1]

The girl's case is more likely to be seen as a family disorganization symptom and less likely to be punished as such. Petitions relating to girls are most frequently made by parents, while those relating to boys are usually by law enforcement officials.[2]

✓ Incorrigibility may stem from sister-sib rivalry. Smith relates a case in which the older sister chose to wear blue, the favorite color of the favored younger sister, despite the color's unsuitability to her own brown eyes and hair. Since the little sister was always dressed in blue, which was becoming to her light complexion and fair hair, the older sister unwittingly adopted the blue garments which seemed to be so successful when worn by her sister. Matters worsened between the two girls to the point wherein the older sister avoided family reunions where the younger sister was to be present and even took a trip to escape being a bridesmaid at her wedding.[3]

✓ Incorrigibility may expand to include actual violence, burglary, arson, even kidnapping. One girl entered a home and abducted a seven-month-old baby which she dropped "accidentally." She kept the baby hidden six hours before returning it to its parents who notified police. The baby was taken to the hospital where it was found to have had a fractured skull, lacerations and bruises all over the body. The girl then led a group of five other girls who committed more than ten burglaries of homes, then set fires to destroy the evidence.

✓ Mother-daughter "feuds" may result in incorrigibility behavior, for among some female delinquents there is a subtle and potent interaction between mother and daughter. In many cases the mother is the person who complains to the police or court. The daughter enjoys being a source of disgrace to the family especially to her mother.

✓ Responding to a mother's provocative combination of nagging

and suspicion, the daughter clutches the suggestive signs of sophis-
tication and uses them to goad her mother. There are no laws
against makeup and clothing fads, but smoking and drinking may
be the obvious next moves. The girl inevitably gives substance to
what were initially groundless suspicions. She may stay out all
night or run away. In either case there are likely to be sex episodes
and often promiscuity. In one way or another the mother learns of
what is happening. The notation on the official papers may be
"ungovernable behavior," "incorrigibility," "truancy from home"
or "immoral behavior".[4]

Incorrigibility may manifest itself in ungovernable temper and
lack of restraint. One girl assaulted her sister's sixty-one-year-old
landlady, striking her with her fist and tearing her clothing, causing lacerations on the woman's face, breaking her glasses and
ripping her coat to shreds. As a reason for this outburst, the girl
stated that she was provoked when the landlady slammed the door
in her face. When arrested she attempted to escape by kicking and
scratching the arresting officers.

It is unfortunate that the terminology embracing offenses committed by girls lacks preciseness in definition. In many respects
"incorrigibility" is a weasel term, a blanket type of nomenclature
that includes other offenses which, to the casual reader, may seem
to be more serious than the term "incorrigibility" itself.

Three authenticated case histories follow, illustrating the facts
involved when the official charge of incorrigibility leads to the
girl's commitment.

Jane M.

Efforts to work with the girl in the community were unsuccessful. Any attempts by the parents to help her resulted in outraged
behavior by Jane and her running away from home for longer
intervals. She would slip out of the window at night and meet boys
and older men at various locations. At times she would engage in
"stripping" from her bedroom window. She later admitted having
had sexual relations with at least thirty boys.

Background information disclosed that the family was deserted
by Jane's natural mother several years before her commitment. It

was reported that the mother had also had a history of incorrigible and runaway behavior as a girl. Speculation was that she was engaging in prostitution at the time of Jane's commitment.

Jane's father had completed the seventh grade. He was employed steadily, earning a moderate income. Jane's stepmother, who is four years her husband's senior, is described as being obese and unattractive. Her marriage with Jane's father was her first. She met Jane's father at her place of employment where she engaged in secretarial work. She is further described as being ambitious, talkative, outgoing and quite proud of her family. The stepchildren seemed to be very fond of her. Jane especially liked her and seemed to take pride in claiming that Mrs. M. was the only mother she ever had.

Jane's family lived in a very nice neighborhood in a newly developed residential area. She has her own room neatly furnished with modern equipment.

Jane and her brothers reportedly had few social contacts while they were with their real mother. After she deserted them they made poor adjustments in several foster homes.

Jane had an ambivalent relationship with her father. She indicated that sexual experiences occurred only when she got upset at home and would leave her family. She was quite confident that she could never adjust in her own home and had ceased trying. She volunteered that she would prefer living in another foster home rather than returning home to her father and stepmother.

Her father and stepmother were of the opinion that Jane had a strong need for punishment and that she was unconsciously identifying with her natural mother. They felt that her commitment to the training school would help her in a protective setting and there she would become more receptive to the expectations of her family and society.

The clinical evaluation at the training school indicated that Jane utilized many strong defense mechanisms and found it difficult to verbalize her feelings about many situations, especially her relationship with her father. It was speculated that a traumatic incident in Jane's relationship with her father contributed to this. She was given an opportunity to have intensive counseling while at the school. She was described as a girl of high average intelligence but initially she refused to attend academic school. She preferred to remain in her cottage to be near the housemother and expressed considerable fear of the other girls when she first arrived at the school. After a short period of counseling, she attended school on a full-time basis and worked diligently. Her relationship with her peers was considered poor. Consequently, she attempted to make friends with the older and more sophisticated girls.

Although progress was made in helping Jane with her deep-seated problems while in the training school, it was felt that out-patient treatment would be more effective.

Anne E.

The offenses leading to Ann's commitment to the training school were incorrigibility and runaway behavior. At the time of commitment, Ann, a 16-year-old white girl, had a previous history of running away from home on five occasions. At one time she stayed away for fifteen days and was picked up in a southern state in the company of two boys with whom she was reportedly an accomplice in a theft. Throughout these runaway episodes she lived either with a girl friend or a boy friend. Her prior contact with the court resulted in her being placed on probation. Her parents were very lax in notifying the authorities of her absence.

The home had been one of much emotional stress. Her father was a heavy drinker and this led to many quarrels between the parents. As a youth, the father had a record of stealing cars and bicycles, drinking and fighting. He left school after the sixth grade. He was the second oldest child in a family of eight. His mother died when he was ten years of age and his father married a young girl within the same year.

Ann's mother is of middle age, three years older than her husband.

Her father died when she was eleven years of age. She was described as an emotional person who cried easily.

The family lived in a small apartment in an interracial neighborhood in a medium-size urban community. The neighborhood was described as depreciated. The apartment was inadequately furnished and housekeeping standards were poor.

There were four siblings living in the home, all of whom were younger than Ann. One sister was living with a maternal aunt. Also living in the same household was the maternal grandmother, who stayed with the family until Ann was five years of age. Because of the grandmother's extreme poor health and her permissive attitude towards Ann, the parents were reluctant to discipline the child, lest the resultant dissension would cause what was described as "spells." The death of this grandmother appeared to be a traumatic experience for Ann, then eight years old, and she began stealing and experiencing increasing problems in school. Ann was admitted to the training school and attempted to give the impression of being frank, friendly and anxious to please. She showed little ability for understanding the nature of her behavior and apparently lacked awareness of the hurt she caused her family.

On one occasion Ann attempted to run from the institution but was apprehended within the hour. She reasoned that her homesickness had caused her to take this action.

It would appear that Ann's grandmother had given her the total needed attention, which she was denied after the grandmother's death. By contrast, Ann's relationship with the parents appeared superficial and without deep, meaningful ties. During Ann's early development period the grandmother was very permissive with her—the school evaluated this fact as adding complications to the already stressful family picture. It was concluded that Ann's acting-out was a reaction of her deep feeling of rejection by her family and her need to establish a meaningful relationship. She was described as being a very attractive girl who related in an open and friendly manner and was very anxious to please.

Esther M.

I, Esther M., was born in April, 1949, in .... Hospital in Chicago Illinois. From that time up until I was about eighteen months old, my life was pretty dull. In my eighteenth month of life things started shaping up, the things that would make me the person I am today.

My mother, Johnnie, was sentenced to Dwight (women's prison) for from one-to-fourteen years for manslaughter, of which she only served eight and a half years. And then I started going from one person to another. The people I remember best were Thelma J. and William S. (common law marriage) who did most of my raising. I was clothed decent and fed more than I should have been, although I had never slept in any bed other than a baby crib, which eventually I outgrew. I was quite accustomed to sleeping on couches with a blanket under me and one over me also. When I was about four, Thelma and William split up and another women come to live with him with only the clothes she had on. Thelma had left hers so they came in handy, but she resented me so she made me do things four-years-olds shouldn't have been expected to do. I wasn't fed right — half dressed, dirty and nasty all the time. My meals consisted of cornflakes and water for breakfast, no lunch, unless it was a handout from someone, and dinner with blackeye peas and corn bread, not one day but every day. There was nothing I could do or say about it. William, who eventually turned into a wine-head, wasn't aware of this. I wasn't quite six when she gave birth to a baby in the house, which I quite plainly saw. The doctor, the nurse nor anyone else paid any attention to me and since there were no doors in the way, I walked in and saw everything.

As soon as the baby was about two months old it was my job to watch it, change its diapers and I was quite frequently left alone with him, so I took it out on him. I used to hold him in my arms and stand in the middle of the floor and let him go. He wouldn't hurt himself but he would cry and end up with bruises, but at that age I had already learn how to lie in order to save myself. I would give some excuse which in the end I was whipped for, but it didn't make any difference, I would have been whipped if I had have told the truth anyway. One morning about two or more weeks later I was on my way to school and Rosealee put her foot in my back and pushed me three flights down the stairs which split my arm open. The stairs was nasty—anybody drifted in the halls and urinated, drank wine and eliminated themselves of any other waste they might contain.

In June of 1955 I announced I was leaving after I had been given a dime and bought a custard with and coming up the stairs

I dropped it, so I was whipped for wasting money and I was fed up I guess, that is if it's possible to be fed up at that age. I had been visiting these people who fed me and washed me and combed my hair, and the last person who did that was Thelma and I was attachd to them. I was having temper tantrums then and I wanted a popsicle. William reached in the freezer and gave me a half of one that had been broken into. I didn't want it, I wanted a whole one so I started crying, screaming and the like and he told me either to stop crying or to leave so I got up and left without the popsicle.

So on this night in June I went and rang their doorbell and the door was opened by Mrs. F. who took me upstairs, Mr. F. came and brought the box upstairs which I had drugged the three blocks from Wells to Orleans. Most of my possessions were bloodstained for someone arguing and someone getting hit with a pop bottle which all the blood squirted on my clothes she had laying in her lap. They never were cleaned until the F.'s cleaned them. From the moment I set a foot in their house my life began—doctors, courts, social workers and parole officers. I was bathed and I made the comment, "No one ever washed my face like that, mama." I readily accepted her as my mother, I guess I needed someone to be attached and she was the only person that treated me like I should have been at that age.

I was taken to court the next Monday and they received legal custody of me. In September I started to school. There was some question as to what grade I should be placed in as it was brought out in the open I for some reason been thru kindergarten twice. In the end I was placed in first grade and I received a double promotion to the third grade. One night when I was coming along pretty good—kind of used to kids sleeping alone, sheets, pretty clothes, going out to dinner and simple little things in life—I got up, dressed myself and tipped out and walked the streets. About two o'clock in the morning a paddy wagon picked me up and took me back after a lot of questions. That was the first night I got a spanking from them and that's about the time when I started going to psychiatrists and psychologists. They were trying to help me find myself and the reason for running away so much. I guess

I was overly curious and at the age of eight I was read and told the facts of life, while I understood very well. They found out my problem mostly was being stubborn.

At this time I had stopped running away so much but now I was developing another problem. In school I couldn't get the catch of arithmetic, so my father made me work on it for an hour which alway's wound up two or three hours longer. His patience was shorter than my mother's and he hollered at me and by having sensitive feelings and being stubborn it made me more determined not to learn (I never did). At ten I had been put in Audy Home and released and I had learned that I liked to steal. I stole from my father's pocket when he was asleep. It was found out from a friend who made a statement about he having a lot of money at school. Of course I was punished. I used to give my sweater's and rings, gloves, anything I had, to some other child who I felt needed it. I never was a sick child. I had the chicken pox and the flue and I also had rhinitis which doesn't bother me anymore, but I used to pretend sickness for attention.

Around my tenth birthday Johnnie, my mother was released and came with another woman to give me a present, a cross and a box of handkerchiefs. Over the years she had corresponded with the F.'s. She had sent crocheted houseslippers, pillow cases and dresser scarves to me which I still have. I couldn't really believe she was my mother—although I knew Mrs. F. wasn't—and so I told her she wasn't my mother. I really started running away then. I said I wanted to live with Johnnie—really I didn't, I just wanted an excuse. This is when I first came in contact with homosexuals. I was pretty quick to catch on. She gave me my first reefer, bootleg whiskey, cigarette, beer and any other thing which might have become a habit with me.

This man named John B. wanted me. My mother had him buying my clothes and every other thing I wanted, although he was married and had a child the same age as my sister and lived in the same building. He didn't like he cared about her finding out. I was going with a butch named Charles who was twenty-five and in a sense turned me out, but I was playing with this man because of Johnnie and push came to shove, he wanted to go to bed with me but I hadn't been touched by a man, boys yes, but a man of his age would have split me wide open, maybe ruined me for life. I had been drinking and was feeling kind of woozy and Johnnie called me in the room and asked me did I want him to "go down on me," which I had heard about but hadn't experienced at that date. I said "no" and walked out. After Charles left—she was there at that time but I didn't tell her what was said—John pretended as if he was leaving but he really just closed the door. I drifted asleep, when I awoke I was naked and he was in this act of oral copulation. I jumped up and ran into Johnnie's room and got into bed with her and she just told John he had better go now, so he picked up his shirt and left. The next day I was sore and Johnnie put some witch hazel on me. I wouldn't speak to either of them. I went to stay with Charles and I let her do it on my own will—this is when true sex life began.

About a week and a half later I ran away and went to the north side over a girl named June whom I had met in Audy home. I stayed there and she cut my hair in a poodle which at that time hung down my back and she shaped my eyebrows. This started me to wearing makeup. The next day I let her mother talk me into giving myself up.

I was sent to Geneva Girl's School and at eleven in July of 1960 this is where I was to learn what I didn't know already. I hadn't finished fifth grade yet—I had flunked and was in the middle of my second semester when I got taken out of school and placed in Audy Home for the rest of the school season, and when I was with Johnnie it was too late to go to school—but I received an eighth grade diploma in Geneva at eleven just for passing the academic test. I stayed in IYC eleven months, not for misbehavior, just because they felt like keeping me. I was there five months before I got in serious trouble for jumping the matron and taking the keys and attempting to run. I stayed in the unit from December seventeen to December thirty. Then I was place back in my cottage with, only an occasional bad report thru the six months that I spent there afterwards. By being around other girls older and more experienced than me, I had completed my education of life in the streets.

I was paroled June 25, 1961. I met a boy named Tommy who I only went with for about a week before he went to prison. I also met Red and Tyrone although I lived with Tyrone and he had a good job, I preferred Red (who was in jail more than he was out). I went to bed with Red but Tyrone was buying my clothes, feeding me and the like, but still regarded me as being too young to mess with. I got pregnant the second time I had sex with Red and this is when I became aware of the different ways to prevent pregnancy and to keep it from continuing. I had a self-provoked miscarriage, using three small brown pills in the head of a Tampax. Of course I was sick and had to be scraped. I stayed out about six weeks and come back August 15, 1961 for running away. This is when I starting acting up good. About two months I was under a heavy dosage of medicine which was stopped when my mother complained I had no will or reason to behave. I spent fifteen months there which was my fault.

I was paroled December 10, 1962. I was paroled to a foster home where the male foster parent tried to go to bed with every girl who came there. His friend, who had his own television repair shop, like me, so I was encouraged to take him for a sucker, which I did. During this time I had sex once with Red again and I got pregnant, which I didn't know, and was told by the lady foster parent to take some turpentine and sugar. My menstrual came down and I had pains and the like but I never did know whether I was pregnant or not.

I got tied up with another man which is the father of my son. I returned February 15, 1963, five days pregnant. I gave birth to a son October 29, 1963, after eighteen hours of labor. I spent six days in the hospital and refused treatment or food. My weight went from 130 to 156 and down again to 129. When I left the hospital I weighed 123 pounds. I was paroled five days later to my foster parents, the F.'s I had to place my son in a foster home, for the F.'s didn't believe in illegitamate children. I ran away again because I was scared to get a six week check-up. I stayed on the run from December 15, 1963 until March of 1964. I returned home in a cab, weighing 109 pounds and suffering from perigastric infection of the stomach lining. I had my fifteenth birthday April fourth, the first one at home since my tenth.

My parole officer and another parole officer took me to a foster home where I stayed only six days. My father came on April tenth and picked my up and took me to Chicago Mental Health Clinic. I talked with a psychiatrist who had tried to treat me before but I had refused treatment and had run away from home all the time. I was signed into the institution, led to a part of the ward and given a blood test and a slight checkup, taken upstairs on an elevator to A ward, given a bed and told to go to sleep. The next day I was given some tests and talked to two doctors and was put on medicine. On the seventeenth I was committed to Elgin. On my arrival at Elgin I took some blood tests, measle shots and a series of other shots. I don't know exactly how many weeks I was on Read or do I remember how I escaped, but I know I did. I had a spat with a boyfriend and got angry and returned. I was put on Read 5 punishment and I work myself out again and plotted an escape which wound me up on C1 north where the tubs are. I had a little dispute with a crazy lady which wound me up in the tubs and tied down and left me with a scar on my left arm from a bite. I had quite a few incidents with crazy people during my stay. I was transferred to B1 north and at first I was given a temporary pass that would let me be on campus from about 12:30 until 2 or similar hours, but with the little skill I do possess—one of them is the gift of gab—I soon talked my way into ground pass, caught a cab and caught a train to Chicago and stayed there until my boyfriend and I got into it again.

On my return I was put on Read again where I met a butch who wrote me and called and talked to doctors, passed me money and came to see me on all four visiting days. This is the woman who I loved and admired, the one who I planned on spending my life with. I was given an absolute discharge. The night my parents were supposed to pick my up I had to call them, they weren't going to come because I didn't act like I wanted to come home. I stayed home overnight. The next day I was with my butch. I had her transport me back and forth from Waukegan to Chicago daily. She acted like she loved and wanted me; I cared a great deal about her.

I was returned to Geneva for shoplifting. She had given my forty-five dollars to buy a leather coat. I messed up the money and knew I had to have an excuse, so I tried to steal a coat. During my stay, from September twelfth until June twentieth, I raised a lot of cane: two fires, two runs, a series of arguments, two fights, breaking windows, destroying garments and Christmas presents (mine and other peoples) and jumping on matrons.

When I was paroled off of Oak I was glad to go. I thought I wouldn't return. I came in contact with people I knew for years who were pushers, prostitutes, pimps and the like. Tyrone, who had become a pimp and was quite successful at it, wanted me to hustle for him, which I never did. After about two or three weeks he knew it would never be and I guess that's when he fell in love with me. I stayed with him three months. Then, because of me still, at heart, wanting Nita, I returned to her.

The next four months were blissful and full of happiness, the only months in my life that was totally happy. When we were a good pair we fought, played, argued and made up. She took time with me and never tried really to hurt me. She had only jumped on me once and that was before I had returned and then it was jealousy who made her do it. I came in contact with a fence who I stole and sold to. I got busted and ran, they caught me. The coat I left behind was Nita's, a Christmas present from me, so I pacified my freedom for her coat. I returned to Geneva February first at the age of sixteen to spend nine to ten months more locked up.

During my life I have been with poor people and rich people. To me the people who have to scrape and scramble to make ends meet are the only people who enjoy life. A person who has money under his or her feet, life is miserable for.

This short autobiography is the life and loves of Esther M.

Geraldine K.

I was born in Chicago. I lived in Chicago until I was 4 years old, then me and my family moved. I went to ...... grade school. I was very close to my parents. I was always mommys and daddys little girl. When I was 11 I noticed my parents were arguing alot but didn't really pay attention cause I was young. Then me and my sister and my mother moved away one day. We still lived in ......

only 6 blocks away from where we moved from. My sister was just
turning 17 so she was able to get a job and help my mother out.
My mother also worked she worked night shifts. So I had a lot
more freedom than I usually did. Because my mother and father
were pretty strict with my sister and me. I started hanging around
with a group of girls like a gang. I started going out quite often.
I still saw my father every week he came and took me shopping and
gave me money.

When I was 13 me and my mother moved to .... My sister
got married when she was 18. When we moved to ...... I was in
8th grade but I wouldn't go to school cause I didn't know no body
in that suburb. So I started staying home every day and never went
out at all. My mother worked all the time so I felt pretty much
alone. I wasn't used to that cause I always had alot of friends
in .... After 4 months we moved back to ...... cause my
mother thought it would be alot better for me. I started hanging
around with this girl that I grew up with. We started smoking
marijuana cause it was something different to do. I got carried
away cause I hadn't had fun in a long time.

Then in December of 72 I met this boy and really liked him
cause he seemed to care about me. It started injecting speed because I saw every body else do it. I was scared, but I figured if
everybody else did it must not be that bad so I did and I started
doing it when ever I had a chance to. Onenight when I stayed out
all night with ...... and some of his friends we were riding
around in a car. We wanted some more speed. And it was late at
night so we robbed a doctor's office. Because we knew of other
people that did it and didn't get caught. So we did. And we didn't
get caught. So we did and we didn't find much up there so we
thought if we got away with that we could get away with something
else. So we tried to rob a drug store. There was snow out then so
we stayed in the car and let one boy go out he must of made alot of
noise trying to get in cause when he came back to the car about
5 squad cars came over to the car. They brought us all to the jail.
I went to the Audy Home and so did one other boy, but ......
and the other boy got bonded out. The judge sent me to a drug
abuse center at Tinley Park. I was to stay till they thought I was

ready to go home. I stayed there for 2 days I couldn't handle it and wasn't ready to accept counseling so I ran, and came home. I had a warrant out for my arrest. About a month later I O.D. they sent me to Lyola University and were going to commit me to Madden. But I told my Mother I wasn't going to be locked up in no crazy hospital, she said I needed some help, some sort of counseling. I told her it wouldn't do me no good cause I refused to accept counseling. About 3 months later they picked me up on a warrant. And they brought me to ISTSG & BA.

I am sorta glad I got committed because I was in bad shape and pretty sick. Because I was getting no medical attention for my hepatitis. And I needed to settle down. So I could quit drugs.

Nancy J.

I was born in Ill. My mother was at the age of 21. On Dec. 6, 1957 in . . . . . . hospital. I stayed with my parents until I started to run away at the age of nine. We have a enormous family so that made it hard for me because I though everyone was against me. While running away I didn't have clothes to ware nor food to eat so that was my first real stage for stilling. I walked into the stores every day and stole food to eat and clothes to ware. Then life seamed hard because I felt I wasn't up with the croud so I started smoking cigarettes and then shortly after started getting high like smoke weeds droping pill and taking acid. When that didn't seem like fun I started snatching puring, braking in houses, gang banging. But as a person I am learning that crime does no pay. I been locked up over at least 10 times. But it was lot of fun as of now life in jail is a terrible thing for a young lady. As of now I will try to be a young sensible young lady and try to stay out of trouble.

Winifred A.

I started getting out of hand when my father died. I was about the age of nine. I was going to a school called . . . . . . The reason I was put out of . . . . . . is because a boy named . . . . . . said he was older than my father. We were in the gym so I got mad and hit him in the head with a bat and my teacher tryed to stop me and I hit her too. So they sent me to . . . . . . School.

Well, I was at . . . . . . School for about one year and I got my

self in some action at ...... School. Well, the school was okey
but I was sick of school because I couldn't stay up in classes.
...... School finally sent me to ...... school.

By the time I left there, I was in more and more trouble. Looked like I was going to Audy Home for a long time. I didn't want
to stay locked up. When I went to court, I was released to my
mother but couldn't stay out of trouble.

I really got into big trouble with a girl named .... She
called me and said that she had a "it" (a gun). She said ...... had
had let her keep it and he said we could take it outside (use it).
So I went up there with ...... and she said for me to put on some
pants and a hat. So I did it to me. We looked like two boys. Went
out the back way of her house so that no one would see us. She said
lets go down town where the action was and hit the Goodman
Show. Well we went down to the Goodman Show but we did not
rob it. We rob a lady in it and we got away. Then we went to
Wards Store and looked at stuff. Wee took some make-up from
there. It was getting late sowe said that we will go home before
it is 12 o'clock because we had to be in before 12 o'clock or we
couldn't go out the next day so we went to the bus and then the
CTA L. We hopped the L but we got busted running down the
line and the man locked us up in the wash room until the party
(patty) wagon came to get us. Well when we was in the wash
room, ... put the gun up under the bowl and said it won't stay
there. So I keep it. In a little bit of time we were at home but are
(our) mothers had to pay are (our) way on the CTA L and had to
take us to court. Before time for court I ran away and went
to ...... house and then kept going to school. The school told
me to come into a room so my mother could talk to me. A man was
there with handcuffs. He put them on me and I went to the Audy
Home. Then I came to Geneva and I'm still here.

The reason of me hitting the boy and teacher is because they
talked about my father. What I mean when I say they were talking
about my father is that the teacher said that you wouldn't be here
if your father was still living. I told the teacher if she would stop
talking about my father she would get hurt. But she keep talking

about it to a boy when she could have been talking to me about it. It all started because of my temper.

Another time I hit my mother but I didn't mean to hit her I was trying to stop her from hiting me but I really didn't mean to hit her at all. The way it started is I was at . . . . . . house and . . . . . . grandmother call my mother and said that I was at her house with some boys and to come up here right now. Nother came up there and open the door and walked to . . . . . . room and said . . . . . . come down to the house because she wanted to talk to me about beening up there with those boys and . . . . She reach out for ne and I duck her and she hit the door and hurt her hand and I was thinking that she was going to hit ne. So I put ny hand up to stop her from hitting ne and I hit her. But I didn't nean to for real.

Eleanor H.

I was born in Mo. I stayed with my Mother and Father. At the age of 5 my mother took me and my sisters and brothers to . . . . I enrolled in school kindergarten. I never got into trouble until I got into the 4th grade. I guess it was because I wanted to be old like my sister. But any way when I turned 13 years old I ran away. I felt my mother wasn't treating me right. 3 months later I joined a gang I was the queen of the baby lady souls'. I started snatching peoples purses. If someone would say something to that I didn't like me and my girls would do them a job as I got older about 14½ I started stealing real heavy (coats). I would go to . . . . . . and steal a coat that cost about $200.00. When I Turned 15 I stopped gang banging but I was still stealing awfully bad plus I was burglarizing too sticking up. It seemed as though I was going out of my mind. I had been getting high ever since I was 13 years old, still is but I'm not on the needle yet. What I mean when I say yet is I don't know what I will be doing at the age of 17. I am 16½ now. I've been caught with 2 sawed off shot guns 4 38's and a 22.

Conclusions

The incorrigibility described in these cases seem incapable of being corrected. The grave dilemma, understated, is how to correct years of negative conditions and influences and channel these lives in a corrective, positive nature. The only hope for these young girls lies in real evidence from the total society that a nation so great cannot neglect those who are discriminated against, poverty ridden and soul-struck.

We see in these stories much evidence of fantasies and much bravado. We see youngsters who, at a very early age, have sensed a world too powerful to tolerate their inherent weaknesses. Therefore, we note individuals who overcompensate in antisocial behavior and have the strong need to continuously rebel against authority and authoritarian individuals. Precipitating factors, well stated by the girls, actually forced these youngsters to act-out to gain any attention or status. Shown in these stories are examples of many persons in the environment of these girls, both marginally and sub-marginally contributing to their deviant behavior. Most of these girls are brought into the world under uncivilized living conditions, while major cultural centers encircle them. Her homosexual experiences were related to her need for love and affection.

REFERENCES

1. Elliott, Mabel: *Crime in Modern Society.* New York, Harper & Brothers, 1952, p. 201.
2. Cooper, Robert: Comparative analysis of the nature of crime and delinquency in girls as compared to boys. In Frank H. Cohen (Ed): *Youth and Crime.* New York Int U Pr, 1957, p. 70.
3. Smith, Henry Clay: *Personality Adjustment.* New York, McGraw, 1961, p. 4.
4. Wattenberg, William W.: Psychologists and juvenile delinquency. In Hans Toch (ed): *Legal and Criminal Psychology.* New York, H, R & W, 1961, pp. 251-252.

CHAPTER 6

THE SEX-DELINQUENT GIRL

T HE BREAKDOWN OF TRADITIONAL SEXUAL mores and the drift and diversity of changing opinion about sexual morality affect individuals in different ways. Differences in sexual orientation and practice, however, may reflect differences in socioeconomic and class standards. For example, Dr. Winston W. Ehrmann's survey at the University of Florida, a five-year study of college youth, indicates that 61 per cent of the men and 91 per cent of the women "draw the line" within conventional moral limits in their current dating behavior.[1] This finding is fairly consistent with Kinsey's surveys of the sexual practices of women, in which he reports class and educational differentials indicating that sexual intercourse itself is engaged in at an earlier age and more frequently among the less educated who, however, tend to avoid the "petting" preliminaries that are so prevalent among college youth.

Ball and Logan, in their research with lower-class girls in a Kentucky state reformatory, tend to confirm Ehrmann's findings. The girls involved in this study were aware of the middle-class norms, knew promiscuity was socially undesirable, were not hostile to such social norms, but were motivated by the desire to maintain status within their own adolescent subculture. The majority of the girls lost their virginity while on automobiles dates and the principal reason given was that they "liked the boy very much." Nearly a fourth of the girls admitted it was the first date. Subsequently, sex was a part of dating as "the boy expected it," or there was "nothing else to do," for fun or pleasure. Other rationalizations included "had been drinking," "would be considered chicken otherwise," or "everyone was doing it." At least 70 per cent of the girls questioned admitted that they knew it was wrong, and all of the girls were slightly below average intelligence. They had dated actively from age thirteen and had no interest in supervised recreation.[2]

Many juveniles, despite rather extensive sexual experiences, may be incredibly naive in many aspects of biological import. Sessions in group therapy with both boys and girls in institutions seem to confirm this observation. Some delinquents have astonishingly childish notions about sex. David Dressler reports an instance of a youthful parolee who didn't drink coffee because "it gets you syphilis." He explained: "Yeah, You drink coffee and you get noivous. coffee leads to smoking, smoking leads to drinking, drinking leads to goils and goils give you syphilis. No coffee for me."[3]

Partly as a reflection of the contemporary cultural accent on sex, the public is easily titillated by accounts of sexual escapades—a fact on which the newspapers have capitalized. Many notorious sex cases have tended to overemphasize sex as an offense. One club of four girls admitted that their activities were devoted to the "seduction of bus drivers." Our culture permits the female to be more demonstrative toward her object of affection, while any open display of affection by men, even the young male child, is discouraged. As compared with male delinquency (stealing, assault, robbery), female delinquency is largely sexual delinquency and running away. The juvenile male delinquent tends to hurt others, while the female delinquent tends to hurt herself.

There are interesting sex differentials that should be taken into account when handling juvenile offenders. A fifteen-year-old girl is more mature than a fifteen-year-old boy. The boy may not know whether he is a man or still a child, but the fifteen-year-old girl knows she is a woman. Girls feel the loss of status with peers more than do boys. Girls are far more dependent than boys on the status furnished by the family, any family, even the "make believe family," so frequently found in informal groups in girls' institutions.[4] If a girl is caught in delinquency, other girls' mothers won't let their daughters associate with the "bad" girl; hence, the female offender has a "bad girl" role. Many sex offenses of juveniles are relatively unimportant and are often due to a fixed morbidity or adolescent experimentation. Although society is upset by the promiscuous girl, the promiscuous boy is regarded with tolerant amusement as only "sowing wild oats." Female delinquency may also be affected by premenstrual tension or postpartum reaction.

The extent of adolescent sexual experimentation by girls, both delinquent and nondelinquent, was noted by Short and Nye as they compared this activity among girls in high school and correctional school. As part of the reported delinquent behavior, 14.1 per cent of the high school girls admitted to have had sexual relations with a person of the opposite sex, while 95.1 per cent of the correctional school girls admitted to the same offense.

In some instances the mother of the girl may be gaining some vicarious satisfaction from her daughter's misdeeds. In one case, the investigating policewoman said the mother greeted the girl the morning after each date with the taunting question: "Are you still a virgin," Who was suggesting what to whom,[5]

In some disorganized areas and families, opportunity for sexual exploitation may include homosexual as well as heterosexual contacts. Influenced by promised financial rewards, boys have been known to aid and even seek out older males, who prefer them as sex objects. There is also the problem of females who use youngsters for normal, as well as deviational, sexual gratification; a practice which is often known to the police of metropolitan areas. Lesbianism may be found at all age levels. According to Short and Nye, 3.6 per cent of the girls in their high school sample admitted having sex relations with another person of the same sex, and 25 per cent of the correctional school sample of girls admitted having had sex relations with another person of the same sex. Only 0.5 per cent of the high school girls admitted commiting this offense more than once or twice, while 12.5 per cent of the girls in the correctional school sample admitted to having had sex relations with another person of the same sex more than once or twice.[6]

As pointed out by Elliott and Merrill, studies of women and girls who were inmates of correctional institutions have shown a large percentage to be sex offenders, whether or not they were committed on that charge. Apparently judges are more apt to sentence women with a record of sex delinquency, irrespective of their current offense. Studies made in this area by Dr. Elliott, Katherine DuPre Lumpkin and Sheldon and Eleanor Glueck from 1929 to 1934 substantiate this statement. More recent analysis of women serving federal offenses at the U. S. Reformatory for Women at Alderson, West Virginia, also bears out this conclusion. Even though none of the women in the Federal Reformatory are committed for sex offenses, about 75 per cent apparently have some record of prostitution.[7]

✓In the run-of-the-mill juvenile court cases, illicit sex behavior is not so frequent. A study of the Allegheny County Juvenile Court (Pittsburg cases) in 1958 indicated that 15.3 per cent of the 604 white girls brought up during the year were referred on sex charges, and 34 per cent of the 267 Negro girls were referred on sex charges, a total of 184 girls in all. In the same period, a total of 352 girls were referred for ungovernable behavior and running away. These three charges comprised more than half of the group. While boys brought to juvenile court exceed girls numerically in the Pittsburg juvenile court, only 8.9 per cent of the boys, as opposed to 21 per cent of the girls, were brought to court on sex charges. Probably such court cases represent only a fraction of the total juvenile sex offenders of juvenile court age in Allegheny County.[8]

Abraham G. Novick has summarized in a most succinct manner how the female delinquent may become almost hopelessly enmeshed in a social maze of cultural expectations and conflicting roles and statutes. Social pressures tend to foster a dependency role for the female; a need to be loved, accepted, protected—best achieved through marriage and a family; a necessity to develop special techniques so that she may cope with her male environment; a tendency to place much emphasis on narcissistic attributes that render her more attractive to men, but which still permit open expression of affection toward members of her own sex.[9]

The following stories of their personal experiences were written by two girls who were committed because of sexual delinquency. These narratives illustrate some of the circumstances which can bring about the adoption of patterns of delinquent sexual activity in response to adolescent and preadolescent conflicts.

Jane D.

I Jane D. was born Dec. 9, 1950, in .... Hospital at 8:45 P.M. My Mothers name is Thelma. She married to a man whose name is James. I have seven sisters and four brothers. My Mother died when I was three years old. I was too little to understand her death. but now that I am going on sixteen I understand and it hurts. I lived out in Silver Park until I was nine, and I dont know very much about my life up until I went into a foster home at ten. I lived in Joliet, Illinois. I hated that place so much but I was scared to tell my caseworker. Her name was Miss H. and she was very nice to me and my sister Peggy. She took us to Riverview and we had a nice time. Peggy and I got moved to another foster home on 89th Street. I hated that one too, the lady was too strict on me and oh, how I hate that.

The Ladys name was Miss E. T. I used to run away from her all of the time. Her sister named Ester used to keep us when she go to work, and everytime I do something she'd tell her. She used to rag me all the time until I got mad and ran away. A very bad thing happened, but I do not wish to tell this because it could get my sister in trouble. I used to be so ashamed of myself 'cause I was so skinny and boys would never talk to me. I know I fell for one boy named Buford. He was real fine. He was likin' me. But he woudn't go with me because of the shoes I wore. They were very ugly. My foster mother made me wear a pair of boyshoes. I was so ashamed until I cried. That's when I thought my world had closed in on me. Then a girl named Nancy had a fight with my sister and made her mouth bleed and I beat the mess out Nancy. But then one day my foster mother had left and my little sister and I let her boy friend in the house. She was kissin' him and I didn't even have a boyfriend and I was thirteen at the time. I used to always stare at people. Some people couldn't stand me because I had long hair. But I was young then and didn't know anybetter. Well after that my girl-friend named Diane took me over to her boyfriend's house and she embarrassed me so bad I cried. Then I ran away and my girlfriend Diane squealed on me to my foster mother and she came to the house and got me and called the police on me. They took me to the Audy Home and I stayed there for three months. Boy, was I glad to get out. Then I moved to 81st. There I met my six foster sisters. So I started school and met friends. At first my foster sisters couldn't stand me 'cause my legs were pretty and I had pretty hair I would always get my men. So then I hipped them to the situation. They used to always go and tell my foster mother I was messin' with boys, but really they were messin' with me. So one day I was jumpin' rope and I had on tight shorts, gym shoes and a blouse. It was kind of short, you could see my bra a little. So a boy named Joe was 16 and I was 14. He came by on a bike and said, "Hey baby, what's your name? You sure is fine." I just blushed and by foster sisters got jealous. He came by my house one day and asked to see me and I didn't want to be bothered with him so I just stayed in the house. Joe was shorter than me but he was cute. So one day I went to the park and he rode me on his bike and asked me to go with him, so I did. Everything went mellow for a while, then we broke up. His gang came around there to fight me and I was willin' and ready, then my foster mother took me to the police station and reported it. After all the trouble, I got the blame for it and I got a whipping. They could see it they laughed but Joe didn't, he just walked away. For a while we didn't speak. One day when I was in the park all of his friends came over there. After that Joe said, "Let's kiss and make up." But we didn't, so after a while we got to arguin' and then after a while we made up. So his friend name Paul wanted to go with me. I wouldn't go with him. Soon I got all them niggers up tight and had them byin' me stuff. Joe was strung out over me, bring me money & food and stuff.

Then I start goin' with a boy name James. He was a ring-a-ding-do. I met him September 28, 1964. He was sixteen at the time and fine as he wanted to be. He had broke his arm one day when he rode me on the bike, and as soon as I got off he got hit by a car. When he started to get up he couldn't move his arm. I felted bad. He got it broke in three places. So after he got out the hosptal, he asked me to go with him. He was finer than he is now. So let me tell you how I happened to go with him. One day I was walkin' down the street smoking a cigarette and I didn't know how to smoke then. His cousin named Ann (a stone whore) started teasin' Karen and I and I felt embarrassed 'cause we could smoke. So the next day

Karen and I were on our way to school when his cousin called me and said, 'Jane, my cousin want you." Then Karen said, "Oh oh, don't go," but I went anyway and Ann said, "Jane this is James." Him didn't hardly say anything, but just stare and I felt panic. So then Ann say she will see him later on. That what she was tellin' James. James said to me, "Hey little girl, are you comin' up to my house this afternoon?" I said, "Yes, and I'm not a little girl." Then I went on to school feelin' good 'cause I knew he was going to ask me to go with him. So he came around there before I went in school and kept lookin' at my legs and face. Then I start showin' off for him and he was talkin' to a boy named Little Larry. He said, "Ain't she fine?" and Larry said, "Sure is." Then I went on in the school. I didin't hear the rest.

So when I got out of school he was on the other side of the street and said, "Wait up," to his cousin, 'cause I was with his cousin. So then he stopped and talked to this girl named Mary and gave her a cigarette. Then Ann said, "Give her one." So James said, "I ain't goin' to hardly have any." But he gave me one anyway. So I went up to his house. Then Ann thought she was slick, talkin' about, "Oh, I'm going to the store. I'll be back." But she just wanted to leave me and him alone. So James he up and said, "Do you go with anybody?" I said "No." He said, "Well, do I stand a chance with you?" I said, "Yes." He said, "Well, in other words, you will go with me." Then he said, "Don't that deserve a kiss?" So I said, "Yes." So he start to kiss me, and I didn't put my arms around him. He said, "Well, damn baby, you're not makin' any effort," so I did. This way this first boy I had ever kiss, and you best to believe I enjoy it, but after we got through I felt very weak. So I said, "James I've got to go home." So he told me to come over his house tomorrow. So I went home and told Margaret about it and she told my foster mother. I was so mad! Then she said she was sorry, then me and Margaret go to be real tight. So after awhile I went to the store and sneaked over to James' house. Then I rang the door bell. His sister answered. I said, "Is him home?" She said, "James Jane want you." He came to the door all sharp and everything. I said, "Hi, and where are you going'?" He said, "I'm going somewhere," but he wouldn't tell where. I had a feelin' he was goin' over another girl's house, but I didn't say anything. So I left and went back home. So the next day I went to his house. It was on a Wednesday 'cause I ditched school that day. So he kissed me, and then awhile after that he asked me a question but I didn't quite understand, but I knew what he was askin' for. I just stared at him. Then he took me in the bedroom and we started to kiss and grind. Then after awhile he started fumbly under my dress. I didn't stop him 'cause I was anxious to see how it felt, 'cause I was a virgin and I had heard it felt good and all of that. So he took his thing out and tried to put it in me but it wouldn't go in, and it hurt when he tried to put it in. So I wouldn't let him do it. We stopped for awhile. So then he asked me to take all my clothes off. I said, "No." Then he finally talked me into takin' them off. I took everything off but my panties and bra. So we got in the bed. Then he kept tryin' to get it in me, but it was hurting so I told him. Then he said, "Baby, I wouldn't hurt you for nothing in the world." I felt good when he said that. Then he said, "Let's get up from here before you get pregnant." So I got up, took a bath, put my clothes on and sit down. So then James came out there buck naked, I started laughing. Then he start laughing and put a towel around him. So after he took a bath he sit down and tried to teach me how to smoke. Then his cousin named Lester came up there and start messin' with me. Then I went home. I met Karen. She said "Jane, I kept callin' you to come on down so we could go to school." Then she start askin' me a whole lot of things. I told her 'cause she's my ace partner. So after that we went home for lunch, came back and ditch school that afternoon. We went up to James' house again. He wanted to do it again. So he start teasin' Karen about callin' me. Then he said, "Let's play wisk," and if he win he gets to do it to whoever he wants to and if we win we don't have to let him do anything to us. So we won a couple of times and lost, but he never did get what he wanted from us 'cause we cheated, and that made him kind of mad. So after awhile we heard a knock on the door. James said it was his mother, so we slipped out the back door. When school let out, his little sister said, "Jane, Jim told you a lie—that wasn't my mother, that was some girls." So I went with him for two weeks and quit him. That love affair didn't last very long. I told by girlfriend to tell Jim it's all over. He just smiled. But really he was mad inside.

But he got even with me, he told people a whole lot of lies on me and I felt so bad. Then I went with his friend named Donald, better known as Poo-a-do. So one day I heard Poo-a-do was goin' to fight James. So I said, "Please don't fight him 'cause I used to go with him." Then Donald told me what James said he did to me. So I fixed him. So Donald kept bettin' on me so I would go with him. I didn't want to 'cause I was still in love with James. So I went with Donald. The next day I saw James. I told Karen to tell James to quit lyin' on me. He told Karen to tell me to kiss his ass. When he said that, everybody start laughin'. I was so mad I start cryin', so when I got in school I saw James. Then I said, "I hate you!" He started smilin' a real sneak smile. Then when I got ready to go to my seventh period class, I met him in the hall. He was in my way so I asked him to move. He was with Donald and them. Then he got me up in a corner and start to grind on me; I pushed him away. He start laughin' and said, "When you're goin' to let me get that cat again?" I said, "I wouldn't even let you touch me." He said, "Huh." Then he touch me. I was so mad. He smiled and went on in the gym. So when I start goin' with Donald I never even seen him. He was a jailbird. I know one day I ditched school and Donald's sister said, "Jane, Donald want you. We started out over to his house and when we got there he was sittin' on the steps waitin' for me. I felt funny 'cause I hadn't seen him in a long time. So he was smokin' and he threw it down. Then his sister started to pick the cigarette up then he said, "Jane, don't be teachin' my sister that." I said, "Donald, I didn't teach your sister that, you must have taught her that." Then the bell rang and I stayed and ditched school that afternoon with him. So then we start talkin' about Ann and some more girls. Donald always thought he was slick. He was always hintin' around he wanted some cat. So I said, "If you're goin' with me 'cause of what I got, you can just forget it, 'cause I'm not getting up off of anything." He said he did have his mind in the gutter. I said, "Well, you just can take it out the gutter." Then his mother came and he told me to go out the back door. It was cool and me like a fool was standing out there thinking he was goin' to let me back in. So soon I sneaked through the alley and went home. As soon as I got home I had a check for ten dollars from my father, and that night I went to a funeral. Then I got home one o'clock. When I got home my foster mother told me the teacher had called and said I hadn't been to school that day. But I lied my way out of it. So around Christmas time I went back with James. I didn't want to go but he made me go back with him. I was walking down the street and he called me. I tried to act like I didn't hear him so I went over there and I said, "James, what do you want?" He said, "Come here." Then he asked to go out with me but at that time I was going with Donald. So I start loud talking him, I said, "Who you talkin' to, Elaine?" I say this 'cause see, one day—this is when I didn't know James and he was goin' with Elaine—I went to see her about seven thirty at night in the winter and as I was goin' up the steps to her house I saw two shadows lyin' down on the steps. It really shocked me. They were doin' it. I said, "God." Then I stood there, just shock. Then all a sudden they jumped up like somebody had hit them. Then I talked to Elaine. I said, "Elaine, if you don't have any respect for yourself, who else is goin' to have some for you?" Right then and there she knew James didn't have no respect for her. So anyway I told James, I said, "You must be talkin' to Elaine 'cause I wouldn't go with you if you put a gun to my head. So he pulled me in the hallway talkin' about, "I can't stand Elaine." I said, "Yea, after you got that cat you can't stand her." He said, "Really." I said, "Now I know I can't stand you." Elaine was hollering in there she said, "Your mama comin'," James just laughed. Oh, excuse, I left out a part. One day I was in school and I called "Moose-Lips." He got mad. He came in my room and told my teacher, he said, "Would you please tell that little girl something before I hurt her? She out there callin' me names and I really don't like that. I was very embarrassed. I never did that again. Well I as I was sayin' before I left out a part. The bell rang and James wouldn't let me out that hallway until I slobbed him and said I would go with him, but I was too mean to say it. I kept tellin' James, I said, "I don't want you." He said, "You know you love me," which I did, but I didn't want him to know it. So I played like I hated him. So when I wanted to go to school he made me ditch it. The he dragged me by my hair and took me up to his house and started kissin' and grinding on me. Well it just so happened James' brother was there and he said, "Man, don't do anything to that girl 'cause you can hurt her." James said, "Man, I ain't goin' to do anything to her." So we just talked the whole thing over and got an understanding. So then I ran away and stayed with my girl friend named Karen.

So when I got caught they took me to Audy Home. I stayed there for three weeks. Then I went to live with my father and I thought I was goin' to like it, but he was just as strict as the others. So when I was on my way home from the Audy Home I saw this boy name Mike. I fell for him at first sight. So that day I went over Dolly's house and he came up there and start hookin' and ask me my name. So I went with him. One night he came over my house and was smokin'. My father said, "Put your cigarettes out. no smoking in this house." So my stepmother came from the store and told him he had to go; I was very disappointed. So one day my stepmother gave me two dollars for allowance and I got a picture taken of me and a record. They blamed it on me that I had took the dollar and I hadn't even taken it. So I showed Mike the picture. First he start makin' fun of the picture. Then I told him about my father. He told not to worry and that he wanted the picture. So one night Mike's sister threw a jam and he got drunk and vomited all over my dress. As much as I like Mike, I had to hit him in the face with the door. Everybody was high except me. Then it was about eleven o'clock on a Saturday, that when I go home. So my father made me sleep in the hallway. But I went up to Mike's house and knocked on the door. His mother answered the door. His mother is mellow as hell. She let us drink and smoke and all that and I was lookin' sharp as hello. So she said, "You father put you out again, come and sleep with Mike's sister." Rabbit (that Mike's nickname) was still asleep and drunk as hell. So I start kissin' all over him and he got sober about one o'clock. Mike's mother made him wash my jumper out and take it to the cleaners and wash the vomit sheets. So about one o'clock Sunday he took me to the Regal. So we got home about ten o'clock. I live on the third floor and he lived on the eleventh. We just talked and talked, then I went home about eleven o'clock. My father came in the next morning talkin' about he was going to whip

me. I said "Yeah." I said, "You whip me, it will be your last whip."
So he didn't touch me.

One day I was on the phone talkin' to a boy name Carl, he's real
fine, and my step-auntie come hang up on me. I called her a black
bitch. She went in the front room and told my father. He came
slapping me. I didn't say anything. I just walked away. Then she
sent me to the store to buy some pop, and I got in the hallway and
stood up and called Mike every dirty name in the book. He didn't
say anything, he just walked away. So the next day I was still mad at
him about my dress and what made it worse, I heard he was goin'
with this girl named Sally. I said, "That did it." So they throw a jam
on the fifth floor and I went down there and Rabbit was down
there and Morris was down there. He's black as hell, but fine o-o-o.
The nigger is fine and built. So he start me to talkin' about Mike
and Mike looked back and said, "What I do?" Mike got the
prettiest black eyes you ever want to see. I fell in love with his eyes
right away.

So Mike made up to me, but I was still mad. So he said, "Baby,
you still mad at me?" I said, "Yea." Then he started kissin' on me. I
said, "If you was as drunk as you claimed you were, you wouldn't
gave Morris a dirty look when he was gettin' ready to kiss me." But
then we didn't get to finish talkin' cause his sister came in and we
had to get out. He called me on the phone the next day and say
something smart. I hung up on him. Then he got smart again, I
hung up on him. So he came down to my house and he just looked
at me. I could tell he was mad as a bull the way he looked at me. I
used to run over him 'cause he never would hit me. So one day, this
is before I went with him, he was play cards with me and Marilyn
and Morris. They're gangsters from their heart. And he keep
lookin' at me. Then that's when I knew he was digging me.

So one day Rabbit took my records from me so I went up to his
house to get them but I was suppose to be with Rebecca, but you
get tired of bein' followed all your life. My father was strict on me
that is why I'm the way I am. He made me like that. Well, anyway,
Rabbit wouldn't give me the records, so I went in the laundry
room. He came in the laundry room and locked it, so I kept kickin'
on the door. He ask me to stop, nicely. No, but I'm going to be

smart and keep doin' it, so he kept askin' me why don't I stop. But I would't, so he got mad and knocked me in a tub of water. I went in the house and changed my clothes. He knocked me in another tub 'cause I said it didn't hurt me. I stayed in the house all that week and I went out on Saturday and I met Mike. He didn't say anything but he grabbed me and ask me where I was goin'. I said, "Is it any of your business?" He said, "What's your business is my business." He said, "I love you and that makes a lot of difference." So he said, "Come on and come in the laundry room so I can talk to you." I said, "O.K." Then he start askin' me for some and I say, "No, especially not in a laundry room." So he kept on begging me. So I started to do it but I heard some footsteps and I heard the key in the door so I didn't do anything, but stood up there and asked them what they want. They said, "Yea, you have been doin' it." I said, "You're just a lier." So my father heard about it. He called me a whore and we got to fightin' 'cause I hate for somebody to call me a whore even if it is true, 'cause I know I'm not one.

Well, anyway, I hadn't seen Mike for weeks so we moved in February to 69th and Western. I didn't like it out there 'cause it was too near 71st where James lived. Anyway, before we move I went to the show with Marilyn and met the boy name Joseph, who lives at 39th street, and Charles, Earl, Mitchell and so on. Anyway, I happened to get the attention of these boys and they came over there and start talkin' to me. Marilyn played hard to get. At the end she lost her man. Anyway, I was talkin' to Joseph and he gave me a cigarette and we was really digging each other.

So Charles was tryin' to go with me to but I stuck with Joseph. He is so handsome. He's got a real pretty complexion but he's a stone winehead. But he so nice, so after I left the show that's all I had my mind on, but I was still goin' with Mike. On Washington's birthday they came over my house, lookin' good as usual. But I wasn't home, so when I got home my stepmother started to argue about, "You know your father don't want them boys comin' over here." So she start to whip me so I took the belt from her and broke the window. Joseph wrote me a letter and asked me why did I lie to him and he said that he still care for me and liked me and want me to keep on writin' him if I could.

Well, anyway, he said he hope to see me during the time of the stage show at the Regal. So I went to his house after the stage show and his mother said he wasn't home, but he was. He said "Hey girl, what's your name?" I said, "Joseph." He said, "what?" I said, "my name is Jane." Then he was so happy. He said, "Wait a minute." He came runnin' down the steps and put his arm around me. I felt so good and he walked me over to the projects and he told me about the time his mother told him to get out and stay out. He walk me back to his house so we could call my aunt so I could spend the night over there ' cause I had run away. So anyway we was just talk, and I saw a police so I said, "Joseph, there's a police." He said they wasn't goin' to bother us but they did. They took Joseph home and me to the police station and I slept all the while I was there. I was just lyin' my ass down. I gave them the wrong telephone number and I just sat there and start laughing me head off.

So that night they took me over my aunt's house and she called my mother and she came and got me and nothing happen. One Saturday she let Horace and Marilyn go see Rabbit and I couldn't go so I got mad, puts on some clothes and walk out the house and didn't come back. Well, anyway, I stole some stockings, stocking holder, candy and shoes and went over Donna's house lookin' sharp, so me and Donna went over Butch's house, that's her cousin, and was eat and dancin' so James' brother was over there. He younger than James.

So anyway he was rappin' that B.S. on down to me, but I wasn't no fool. He was beggin me to go with him, but I wouldn't. So we went to get some whiskey for Butch's sister. Everywhere I go seems like Mike would follow, and he kept followin' me, byin' me stuff and all that. The reason I wouldn't go with him was 'cause I thought he was like James. But I wasn't takin' any chances 'cause I didn't want him to hurt me like James did. But I couldn't stand Mike and was, and still is, in love with James. Like they say, when you talk about the devil, here it comes. Anyway, I ran out the house with Butch's leather jacket on. He came after me, and as I was goin' to the store I saw James come across the street. I couldn't believe my eyes, he looked so shabby and raggedy. When James saw me, I looked so different he didn't even know me, so I got smart with him. He start to chase me. Then he ask Donna he said, "Who's that?" She said, "Jane." He sound very surprise like he didn't know me. So he gave everybody a cigarette but me. So I cursed him out. He didn't say nothing. he just looked at me. So we was walkin' and Donna and them left me behind and when James keep lookin' at you that means he's up to no good. So he kept lookin' at me. Then when we turned around to go under the viaduct he grabbed me and start talkin' about, "What you doing out here?" I said, " I didn't come to see you so why worry." Then he said, "You probably ran away," in which I did but I played it cool. So he looked at me real funny and kissed me and whispered, "I love you Jane." Then he said, "Come with me." I said, "No." Then we started wrestling, then I screamed and I saw this boy pass by. His name is Clifford, but I didn't know he was a friend of James'. He came and start talkin' to James, then they grabbed me and dragged me to this basement where a whole lot of glass was and they tried to rape me, but I screamed. Clifford took my panties and said if I didn't give him any that he would beat me up, but I didn't care. Now I used to go with James and he's goin' to sit up there talkin' about, "Give my friend some." "Just cause I give you some that don't mean I have to give him some," and I called James a no-good nigger, and I could tell that hurt him 'cause he looked at me and walked out. Anyway, Clifford's mother made him let me go and I was cryin'. Then Clifford came up in my face with some B.S. like this, "are you mad?" I said, "You damn right I'm mad! I sure in the hell ain't glad?" Then he started to give me a comb to comb my hair. I didn't even want it, and I never did get a chance to pay back James and Clifford for tryin' to rape me, but I will. In due time they will pay.

So I saw Donna and I start cryin', so a boy named Ted said, "Let's go find James so I can beat the hell out of him." But Al said, "No, 'cause you'll have all the "Cobas" on your back." Al is fine as he want to get. So that night I stayed over Donna's house. I went back over Donna's house that Saturday. We jammed. Ted got drunk. We was playin' records and Al was up there at Tony's and she was suppose to have no company. So Al was up there and I had his hat. So her mother was comin' and they ran out the back door.

See, Al didnt like Tony, he was just usin' her to get what he wanted out of her. So, anyway, Tony was just kissin' Al and her mother caught them. She didn't do anything, she just talked to them. Then we ate and listen to records.

Then this boy named Nelson wanted to go with me. I went with him and quit him the next day. I didn't like him, I just went with him for his money. But you know how something be on your conscience. Well, I just broke up with him. He was goin' to take me to the show but I just said, "Forget it." So he kept trying' to talk to me but I wouldn't listen. So he just give up. So that Sunday night I was in the store and some fine-ass boys was in there and then Donald came in there. So Donald didn't know me so he said, "is that Jane?" And the first thing he said was "Where is my picture?" I kind of stuttered a little 'cause I had torn his picture up, and I know he was mad. So he came over there were I was and said, "Give me my picture." I said, "I torn it up." He said, "What?" then he start chasin'. Then he caught me and then he said, "Jane, I want you so bad, but the main point is if you want me."

Leslie W.

My name is Leslie W. I was born in 1949 in Chicago, Illinois, on the West side. I don't remember my father 'cause my mother divorced him when I was six weeks old.

I don't remmeber (too) much of my childhood. But my troubles started at the age of nine and a half. I was going to William H. Smith School. There was a boy I was crazy about named James. His sister's name was Linda. We all went to school together. I enjoyed their friendship. Linda use to talk back to her mother and never listened to what she said. So I decided to do the same thing, but my mother made me listen. Linda and I was always in trouble at school, so that made my mother have to come to talk to my teacher.

My mother made her mind up to move away. When she moved, she moved too far for me to go see Linda. My new school was Suder. I never got along there. One day at school I got into a fight. After the fight I went home and got my mother's little knife. The girl and I got to fighting again and I cut her. She went to the hospital and stayed three days. After she was released, we went to court. The judge said since I was only eleven years old and was never in trouble before, I could go home. That was my first big trouble.

They took me out of Suder and they made me go to Motley Haven Adjustment School. I really didn't mind' cause it was all girls and you could smoke.

I enjoyed school for awhile. One day, as I was waiting for the bus, there was this man who somehow made me keep my eyes on him. Every morning we were waiting for the bus together. He was on his way to work. We began to talk to each other. He was so nice to me. He dressed very neat. I used to daydream that we were married. Finally I got him to tell me his name, Robert, age 27. He worked in Harvey, Ill.

Robert was my world alone. We started to meet at the Four-Star show. We would spend hours there, and in the summer we went everywhere. The first time I went to his apartment, I was twelve years old and he wanted to give me my birthday present. He gave me a two-piece suit and a watch. I thanked him. At home my mother was upset 'cause it was after 10:30 when I got there. I told her about Robert. For a whole year, almost, she didn't know I was going with a man. When she said he was too old, he would be locked up, I ran away. I stayed two days. After I return home Robert said he would never see me again 'cause of my mother. My mother had some pills on the table. I took seventeen sleeping pills and sixteen pain pills. I wanted to die more than anything that night. After that I don't remember 'till I woke at Cook County Hospital. They had to rush to save my life. Three weeks later I was fine.

My mother signed some papers to have me go to an institution. I stayed there eight days. On the eighth day, the doctors let me go home 'cause they said there wasn't nothing wrong with me that my mother couldn't handle. That night Robert came and picked me up and said he was leaving for my sake. I ask him not to go.

On my 13th birthday I went out with Robert. Some of my friends started to drink, so I did. We were drinking Johnny Walker Red Lable. Everyone was talking about sex. We were at Denise's house. I was surprised to hear my friends talk about this kind of mess. I wandered how this thing was like? Why haven't Robert and I had sex relationship before? Or wasn't I sexy enough? I was beginning to get sick from that Johnny Walker, so Robert took me away from the party. He was mad 'cause I had been drinking. He said he couldn't take me home like I was. So we went to where he lived. There I asked him about these three questions that ran into my mind. He took me into his arms for the first time and kissed me like I was a woman.

The thread had come out of my pants so he gave me a needle and thread out of the bedroom. He had a nice clean house. He had three big rooms. It was so cute. I went into the bedroom to sew my pants. I asked him to come in to talk to me. So he asked me did I know the meaning of love. I said, "Yes." He told me that he loved me. He came and sat close to me and our lips met agin. And then, somehow, his hands begin to move all over my body. And I became too weak to sit up, so I reclined a little. He was so tender to me. I can't write down on this paper my feelings toward what happened. But afterwards I begin to cry and he took me into the living room and said he was sorry. I was bleeding and I thought I was going to have a baby, so I begin to cry 'cause I didn't know anything about life.

He took me into his arms and set down to explain a few things to me about the facts of life, about sex relationship, and marriage; also that it was wrong for him to touch me—he could go to jail for that.

I wondered why my mother didn't tell me about sex and different things. Why was he telling me these things? After that I went into the bedroom and cried, 'cause I wanted to be loved by a man but not with sex.

After I got home the next morning my mother beat the mess out of me. She then took me to the doctor to be checked. The doctor's report was, "Yes, She has had something to do with a man."

I hurted my mother so bad, she cried 'cause she knew that her wish would never come true—for me to finish high school. She wanted to know who was this man. I wouldn't tell her. She never thought Robert and I were still together.

I ran away from home about twice and always came back. The second time I returned home, my mother had found out about Robert and I. It was about 7:30 P.M. She told me to wash dishes. As I was washing a fork, she went to hit me. I turned and the fork went into her arm. I ran to the corner to call the police. When the police came, they took me to the Audy Home and my mother to the hospital.

The next morning my mother came to get me to take me home. Robert came to my house and we talked about my trouble.

January the 17th, they wrote a special delivery letter to my house to come to court. January the 18th, I went to court. They send me to Illinois Youth Camp. I was so hurt. I can't even say how my mother's feelings was. After coming to Geneva, I stays on Rec. II for three weeks, then got transferred to Willard. At Willard I learned about girls going with girls. I got into the H.B. going with a girl name Dolores, but my heart and soul still belonged to Robert.

I stayed three months and one week on Willard and I went to Faith. I stayed 4 months on Faith and went home. Robert sented me a pair of black shoes and purse. I went home September 17, 1963.

They gave me a welcome-home party, as I was 14 years old when I got out Geneva. At my welcome-home party I prayed to God 'caust he had took care of my mother and the only man I loved. My mother had bought me seven suits. Robert had me a coat and new underclothes.

My P.O. told my mother I was to start back to Motley. We had a wonderful time together, Robert and me. After the party we went for a walk. He told me about a woman named Louise that tried to take my place. But I didn't care 'cause I was home. He had waited for me eight long months. Life was wonderful to me again.

October 10, 1963, I became sick. My mother ask me had I been on my monthly period, but I never answered her. Robert told me I was going to have a baby. I went to school telling everyone.

My Counselor wrote my house to ask my mother to please take me to Illinois Research Hospital. The doctor told me he had to take more tests, he wasn't sure, to come back in six more weeks. I stopped school. My P.O. came to my house. I told her. She was so nice. I was so happy but my mother was so unhappy, 'cause she knew I would never finish school now.

Six weeks later I went back to the doctor. He told me I was going to have Robert's baby. I was so very happy. In the meantime, at home, I wasn't getting along with my mother at all. I couldn't stay there or I would went stone crazy. So my P.O. gave me her permission to live with my aunt. I kept the children for her while she worked. The money I got, I saved. My P.O. was so sweet and understanding.

At 8:30 P.M. on May 17, 1964, my water bag burst. On May 18, my baby was to be delivered. I stayed in labor twenty-four hours. At 10:00 that night, I was took into the delivered room. At 10:05 I found out I was to have twins. At 10:32 one of my twins was born, at 10:41 the other one. They was nine minutes apart. But one died. Why? I guess I will never know. They never told me. The one that died was named "Pandora." The one that is living was named "Senora." "Precious" is a nick-name; cause she is so precious to me.

Pandora weight 3 lb., 14 oz., Senora weight 2 lb., 12 oz., I had to sign some papers to give them permission to keep Senora for treatment til she weigh 5½ pounds.

After being at home for about two weeks, I had to go back 'cause of hemorhaging. I almost died. I stayed three weeks in the hospital.

The day for me to bring my precious daughter home, my mother and I was so happy. Robert was so happy to have her home. Everyone was happy that year of 1964. I never realized that 1965 would bring unhappiness for me. I came back to Geneva for PROSTITUTION.

My daughter needed some milk, so I got it. I didn't ask the man or put myself in a space that he knew what I wanted. Robert had made me upset, so I had asked him never to come see the baby. My mother was gone and I had nowhere to turn. This man told me if I talk to him he would give me ten dollars. I explain my troubles, so he said with the ten dollars I could go get the baby milk. I didn't know he was a well known pimp. So I went to this apartment and he ask he to sit down, so I did. All of a suddenly the police came, and took me downtown for prostitution. After I real what was happening, I gave the name as Delores. They found out my name and that I was from Geneva. I had stayed out of trouble and Geneva for one year and four months.

I returned to Geneva January 11, 1965. I was almost crazy thinking of what my mother and Robert would say when they found out. I stayed out here six months. I was always in and out of trouble. I had over forty reports.

I went home July 14, 1965. Robert and I went to the beach and talked our life over. We were ready to get married. But I met this man named Johnny. We begin to go out and I knew it would be trouble if Robert found out. When I told Johnny we were only friends, he got upset. We begin to fight. After a while he told me I was a fugitive. I told him his mother was a fugitive and he hit me. I begin to get upset so I went into the kitchen and started throwing dishes and pots and pans. The police got into the act. I went to the hospital and then to the Audy Home, from the Audy home to Geneva. I've been out here two months already. When I get home, if Robert still want to marry me, we will be married the same week I come home. This is 1966. My last year of trouble?

In order to analyze the behavior of sexually delinquent girls, one must first have some understanding of the "normal" stages of sexual development which are a part of the maturation process of all children. The conflicts which accompany the various stages of sexual development and the ways in which the child learns to cope with, influence the patterns of behavior it adopts. Furthermore, in relation to these, the child's perception of itself, its parents and human inter-personal relationships are formed.

In early childhood, when the child is three or four it usually experiences what is called the oedipal conflict. It is a phase during which the child becomes aware that her parents have a personal love of which she is not a part. Prior to this, she has only been aware of the close mother-child relationship. With the recognition of the father in its life and the child begins to fantasize that she can compete with the mother for the love of the father. This is the first unconscious sexual attraction which a child experiences.

This conflict is usually resolved when the child must face the fact that, although the father loves her, she cannot take him from the mother. She finds that his love is not sexually motivated and that he acts with the mother in a "caring, protective way" toward her. Then, she learns to respect and love him as a "caring adult" and she places this love in a category of "father love" which is different from "romantic love" as it is not contingent upon or affected by her actions or attractiveness. The father becomes a model for her to use in her choice of a sex-love object (boyfriend and/or husband) when she is older.

However, as she reaches puberty and begins to undergo physical changes accompanying sexual maturation, her earlier conflicts and feelings are usually reconsidered because of her uncertainty about this new adult sex role that she's about to enter. The earlier insecurities, as well as the unconscious hostility, anger and sense of failure and inadequacy engendered by her earlier failure to win her father, cause her to doubt her femininity and her ability to succeed as a female and be found desirable by males.

Usually, the girl works through these insecurities by learning social skills and successfully experiencing acceptance and popularity with her peers. This acceptance reassures her that she is capable of filling the adult female role. As she gains confidence that she will be able to participate in heterosexual relationships and eventually fill the role of wife and mother, and begin to develop more maturity, she is able to make judgments as to the standards of behavior which she will set for herself. Feeling that she is an adequate female, she can incorporate socially acceptable modes of behavior as her other needs for belonging are met in other areas of her life.

In the case of Leslie W., we find a girl who has never known her father, because the parents were divorced shortly after her birth. Apparently, the mother never remarried and so Leslie had no other male as a father substitute. Consequently, it appears that she did not experience the electra conflict in early childhood. Instead, the mother tried to fill both roles, and it is suspected that she was somewhat overprotective of the girl. For example, when Leslie made friends with children who did not obey their parents and began to imitate their actions in school, causing trouble, the mother moved to a new neighborhood.

While the mother probably thought this would help Leslie, she apparently was not able to help the girl in her adjustment to the new environment. Leslie states that she could not get along there and was always in fights. She obviously saw the move as an attempt on the part of her mother to break up her one close friendship upon which she strongly depended. The fact that she tried to imitate her friend's behavior reveals that she was somewhat immature and depended strongly upon others for guidelines for her actions. This suggests a somewhat weak ego development and a limited concept of herself as an independent person. Often, overprotected children fail to gain a clear picture of themselves and their capabilities and, therefore, lack the confidence to make decisions, even small ones, on their own. Such persons are easily led by others.

It seems that the mother was concerned about Leslie though, because she then sent her to an adjustment school. However, this action could also indicate some underlying rejection of the child and a desire for someone else to take over the responsibility for her behavior. She apparently did not feel strong enough to cope with the child and her problems.

Leslie's attraction for Robert occurred as she approached puberty. Since she had not encountered and resolved the electra conflict earlier, this probably was her first unconscious sexual attraction. She sought the same kind of love, and attention that a small child seeks from her father. She wanted to know that she was "special" to him.

Since he was twenty-seven years old, he was approximately the age of her father, and his initial relationship was that of a father or older brother. However, either he was extremely emotionally immature or retarded, to encourage this eleven year-old-child in her fantasy. His gifts and constant attention only prepetuated her infatuation.

When she told her mother about Robert (another indication of her basic immaturity and naiveté and was told that we would be "locked up," her impulsive running away from home and her attempted suicide confirm both her immaturity and her lack of self control. Unable to tolerate her wishes not being granted, she responds to frustration with impulsive action, oblivious to possible consequences.

Once more the mother attempted to get outside help by committing her to an institution for psychological evaluation; another act which Leslie could interpret as rejection.

It was not until she was thirteen that she was even consciously aware of or curious about sex. At that time, she was also extremely upset by the fact that her mother had never helped her to understand this aspect of life. Robert could have helped her to accept and cope with the normal insecurities which she felt then if he had remained in the role of a "caring adult" and father substitute. However, his introduction of sexual activity into their relationship only served to confuse her more.

Her mother's reaction to the discovery that she'd had sexual intercourse, as well as the physical punishment she imposed, served to confirm, for Leslie, the fact that she'd disappointed her mother completely and that the mother no longer had any faith in her. This total lack of warmth and understanding from her mother only made Robert's love and attention seem more important. She saw him as the only source of gratification for her strong, unmet dependency needs. Because of this, she began to rail against her mother, as she viewed her as an obstacle to her happiness. Unconsciously, she also probably resented her mother for failing to meet these needs more adequately. When she acted-out in anger, hurting her mother, she felt deep remorse and called the police for help.

It is interesting to note that both the mother and Robert supported her during her stay in the training school, sending gifts and giving her a welcome-home party. It appears that the mother also had dependency needs and could not tolerate rejection from her daughter. Instead, she bought gifts and seemed to accept her daughter's relationship with this older man. As a consequence, Leslie did not mature much from her experiences away from home. She only waited for the time when she could return to the old situation with Robert.

While Leslie was extremely young, naive and immature, her reaction to her pregnancy at fourteen suggests that she might also be intellectually retarded. She did not seem to be aware of the social consequence or to comprehend that unwed motherhood is unacceptable behavior in our society. Instead, she joyously announced the fact to all of her friends in school.

Once more the mother rejected her and she went to live with an Aunt until the birth. However, she still continued to see Robert. After the birth of her twins, the mother again relented and she returned home with the surviving baby. Since Leslie still had Robert and her mother to depend upon, she really did not have to cope with the consequence of her behavior, as they both helped support and care for the child. She could still remain a dependent little girl.

Leslie's behavior since that time reveals that she has gained relatively little in maturity, even though she has undergone various traumatic experiences at an extremely young age. It is suspected that her intellectual limitations will always impede her ability to make wise and appropriate judgments. Furthermore, her lack of impulse control will lead her into further difficulties unless she marries Robert and he gives her constant direction, accepting all responsibilities and making all decisions for her. However, since he also sounds intellectually limited and immature, it is unlikely that Leslie will remain out of trouble.

The girl does not appear to have a delinquent orientation. However, she has not been given sufficient guidance and consistent structure to learn socially acceptable ways to operate in keeping with her limited intellectual capacity.

Conclusions

It appears that some juveniles who engage in inappropriate sexual behavior usually do so because they see it as a means to gain acceptance and love. Usually, when a girl is unable to gain a sufficient degree of acceptance from her home and peers, she seeks to deny this rejection by engaging in sexual acts which she fantasizes to be an expression of another's love.

Few of these girls seem to adopt this pattern because they are particularly driven by sexual desires. These acts only serve to offset (for the girl) inadequacies which she is convinced that she possesses. Unlike the runaway, who uses avoidance in response to her conflicts and frustrations, the sexual offender acts-out to prove that her basic feelings are inadequate, and to gain a temporary release from frustration through appearing to be desirable and wanted. All of these girls are unsure of their femininity and fearful that they cannot fulfill society's expectations of a woman.

REFERENCES

1. Ehrmann, Winston W.: Influence of comparative social class of companion upon premarital heterosexual behavior. *Marriage and Family Living, 17*:48-53, 1955.
2. Ball, John C., and Logan, Nell: Early sexual behavior of lower-class delinquent girls. *J Criminal Law and Police Science, 51*:209-214, 1960.
3. Dressler, David: *Parole Chief.* New York, Viking Pr, 1951, p. 144.
4. Novick, Abraham G.: The female institutionalized delinquent. In Donald Scarborough and Abraham G. Novick, (eds): *Institutional Rehabilitation of Delinquent Youth.* Albany, Delmar, 1962, pp. 158-170.
5. Wattenberg, William W.: Psychologists and juvenile delinquency. In Hans Toch (ed): *Legal and Criminal Psychology.* New York, Holt, 1961, pp. 251-252.
6. Short, James F., and Nye, F. Ivan: Extent of unrecorded juvenile delinquency, tentative conclusion. *Journal of Criminal Law, Criminology and Police Science, 49*:296-302, 1958.
7. Elliott, Mabel A., and Merrill, Francis E.: *Social Disorganization,* 4th ed. New York, Harper and Row, 1961, p. 157.
8. Ibid, pp. 157-158.
9. Novick, Abraham G.: op cit., p. 160.

CHAPTER 7

THE PROBATION-VIOLATOR GIRL

P ROBATION FOR THE JUVENILE OFFENDER is a form of court-dispo-
sition of the child following his adjudication. Although it is
a nonpunitive method of treating offenders, it should not be inter-
preted as leniency or mercy. In England and in the United States,
probation developed out of the various methods for the conditional
suspension of punishment, as attempts to avoid the cruel precepts
of a rigorous criminal law. Among these Anglo-American judicial
expedients, the direct precursors of probation, are the so-called
"benefit of clergy," the "judicial reprieve," the release of an offender on his own recognizance and the provisional "filing" of a
case. However, probation is America's distinctive contribution to
progressive penology, because the development of probation has
been entirely statutory, insofar as the system is an expression of
planned state policy.[1]

In deciding a case involving a girl who is not insane or feeble-
minded, most juvenile or criminal courts will adopt one of the
following alternatives: (a) return her to her home on probation,
(b) refer her to such welfare services as exist in larger cities, (c)
place her in a boarding or foster home, (d) send her to a correctional house or (e) confine her to jail. For chance offenders and for
first offenders, it is generally believed that the most sensible disposition of the case is to return the girl to her home on probation,
under court supervision. There are many advantages of probation
as compared with commitment to an institution. As detailed by
Reineman, probation is an individualized form of treatment; it
applies the methods of social casework; it leaves the child in his
own home surroundings; it enlists the help of community re-

111

sources; it is not considered punitive and therefore is free of social stigma and, as in the case for probation of adults, it is much less expensive than incarceration.[2]

The term "probation" is derived from the Latin "probare" (to test on approval) and was first used by a Boston shoemaker, John Augustus, who tried to salvage defendants who were found guilty in court in the era 1841 to 1858.[3] Augustus seemed to have taken the term "probation" from Puritan theology; that period of life before death as trial and training to qualify the candidate for heaven, according to Chutes and Bell, who cite this inscription:

> In memory of Frederick, son of Mr. Thomas Jackson and Mrs. Lucy his wife, who died March 15, 1778, aged one year and five days. O Happy Probationer! accepted without being exercised, it is thy peculiar privilege not to feel the slightest of those Evils, which oppress thy surviving kindred.[4]

Probation attempts to deal with offenders as individuals; its social principle is to keep these persons out of reformatories and with their families. Probation is a humanitarian method of administering justice. It is, in large measure, a counseling service which emphasizes attitudes of friendship, helpfulness and sympathy. David Crystal points out the significance of family casework in probation. Caseworker, whether in an authoritative or voluntary setting, involves the same basic tenet: that is, to help the girl, involves consideration of relationships within the family setting.[5]

Not every girl adjudicated a delinquent is eligible for probation. There are no real criteria for use in deciding upon probation; it is a matter of grace and not of right. In many states probation is impossible to obtain if the offense is "repugnant" to society, such as offenses against morals or against the government. In Illinois, for example, the offenses of murder, incest, rape, perjury and arson preclude consideration for probation.

Most probation laws provide that the probation agency make a presentence investigation and prepare a report for the court, although the judge is not bound by law to consider the report. The defendant, as a rule, cannot view the report made by the probation officer, nor can he offer testimony in his own behalf. For these and other reasons, the use of presentence investigation reports and recommendations for or against the use of probation as a part of the court process raises some serious issues concerning "due process".[6]

It has been estimated that it takes about three years to rehabilitate a serious child offender, at a cost of several thousand dollars. But, it will cost society even more to retain the same child in a state training school, from which she may emerge more at odds with society than ever. Therefore, few steps would be more economical—as well as beneficial on other grounds—in the improvement of the administration of criminal justice, than the wise extension of probation and the raising of the quality of probation services.

However, for some children and youths in trouble, probation does not appear to be an appropriate practice. To return to her home and neighborhood, a girl of any age who has become habituated to delinquent practices or who has deep-seated maladjustments or whose delinquent behavior springs from brutality or immorality at home or from the breakdown of satisfactory relationships in the family, may involve a disservice to the girl herself, to society and to the cause of probation as well.

As indicated by Ruth S. Cavan, the child placed on probation remains in the community, usually in her own home, and carries on the normal activities of children of her age and sex. Although there may be a slight stigma connected with being on probation, it does not condemn a girl as a delinquent as does commitment to a correctional school. The Children's Bureau defines probation as a "process of helping the girl accept and live with the limitations required by society by developing her potentials".[7] A more limited definition is that the purpose of probation (or function of the probation officer) is "to help the offender comply with the order of the court".[8]

Unfortunately, the way probation is practiced differs in various courts and in different states; therefore, it is impossible to estimate accurately the total number of children on probation in the United States. The number must be several times the number of correctional school graduates, which approximates thirty thousand annually. Lowell J. Carr calculates that if one were to guess that sixty-five thousand to one hundred thousand children are placed on probation each year, it would not be an overstatement of the facts. In a summary analysis by Ralph W. England, Jr., of probation and post probation studies, it appears, from the available research, that probation is an effective correctional device on both juvenile and adult levels.[9]

Probation is an enlightened attempt to cope with a crisis in the life of an offender who posseses rehabilitative potential. It is often misunderstood and underrated by the public because the press coverage is so frequently negative. Probation is less dramatic than commitment to a state training school, and neither probation officers nor successful probationers make "good copy." Ideally, probation services are dignified. Probation is social casework with the power of the law behind it. It is the only really promising rehabilitative technique for use with violators of the law.[10]

An analysis of the girl probation violator is most difficult because she does not present a particular or distinct pattern of behavior. In the probation process, a variety of offenses can bring about commitment if one engages in these activities while on probation. Consequently, violations may include truancy, sexual delinquency, incorrigibility and runaway behavior or a combination of several of these. The commitment results because it is obvious that the individual is not responding to this type of service and apparently is unable to become rehabilitated in the relatively unstructured probation situation.

Most of the girls who violated their probation did not appear to have any insight into their behavior. The most common characteristics detected in the stories written by probation violators, were an awareness that what they had done was "bad" because they did not obey their parent or guardian, and a general lack of respect for their probation officers. While there was no evidence of strong dislike for them the girls, in general, were little affected by the words and counseling of the probation officers and usually attempted to manipulate them. Apparently, the relationship was not constant or close enough to fulfill whatever needs these girls were attempting to meet.

The following stories will give the reader a clearer picture of the varities of behavior which led to commitment as probation violators.

Ann J.

When I was about eight years old, my mother went to school to see how I was doing. When she got to the school she saw my teacher and asked her how I was doing. The teacher said I was her "little angel" and that I didn't get into any trouble whatsoever, and my mother felt real proud of me and I got real good grades. When I was about ten years old, I got a little worse. My mother had to come to school 'cause I had a fight with one of my classmates. When I started getting bad grades and getting into fights about every week, I never got suspended for it, and then I started taking advantage of that and started fighting more. My mother kept coming up to school for mostly the same purpose. When I got punished for it, I blamed it on my teacher. I was so afraid of my teacher writing a note to my mother and asking her to come to school to have a conference with her. I use to come home very day from school and I never skipped school for nothing in the world unless I was sick. I use to love to get in trouble when I was in fifth grade, but I use to be afraid of getting punished for it.

When I was in sixth grade, which was last year, I alternated and I started being good and getting good grades and comin' home from school. I think my mother had to come up to school about twice. I never broke curfew or nothing like that nor disobeyed my mother like I did a little while after. I use to go to shows and parties and come back before dark. It got dark at about seven or eight o'clock. When I was of that age, I had never stolen anything in my whole life, and I never will steal anything for nobody or myself. I also use to go to church every Sunday. I didn't never miss a Sunday unless my mother was sick and my mother is very healthy, and I hardly ever got sick.

When I was in seventh grade, I was good for half of the semester and for the other part I was sort of bad because I started breaking curfew and skipped school and got sent to the Audy Home and then I got put on probation. Then I started leaving the house without permission and I started getting involved in gangs and a lot of fights. I started hanging around real bad girls and I started getting put out of all my classes. I also got good grades for the first two marking periods and bad grades for the last two. When I was in school, we got a new girl in our room and I became her best friend and she skip school. She used to hit teacher back and I sort of like caught on to that — I started skipping school and hitting teachers back. So really, I started being bad — staying out late and destroying school property and I put all of that on myself. I use to talk back to my grandmother and mother and I use to fight my sisters. I use to throw bottles at my sisters and scar up our tables, and it was 'cause of me being bad. I just didn't do anything right then.

The reason why I was in trouble was because I started hanging around with the wrong people and letting them tell me what to do — stay out with them and skip school with them. Then I started telling my mother stories when she ask me what I skip school for, or something like that. I use to get money a lot until I started being bad, and she cut everything short. I hardly ever got anything when I was bad, and that made me feel that my mother didn't like me, but she soon told me why. When I asked her for some money, my mother said that the reason why we didn't get along and why I didn't get any money is because I disobeyed and stayed out much too late. After my probation officer told me I was headed for Geneva, it seemed like I just didn't pay any attention whatsoever.

In May, 1966, I went to court and my judge retained me and I stayed in the Audy Home three weeks. In June I went to court again and the judge said, "Illinois Youth Commission," which I thought was an organization, and where people came to my house to discuss all my problems, and I asked my probation officer, "What was that?" She said, "Geneva," and I got a little upset, but my probation officer had warned me and warned me to come home from school and call her every day at 3:30. I called her everyday but I left the house as soon as we got through talking. My probation officer heard about our gang that I was in, and she told me I was headed for Geneva, but I just didn't pay her any attention. I hurted my mother and I hurted myself. I came home about 10:30 and my mother was lying on the couch crying and I knew what was wrong without asking my mother. I felt **real bad** and I said to myself that it was too late for me to straighten up because I had to go to court the week coming up, and it didn't matter much to me. So I stayed out late because I wouldn't stay at the house. I felt like crying that night because I hate to see my mother cry for something like that. I was sorry afterwards and I told my mother this would never happen again, and she accepted it.

Apparently, Ann had learned, at an early age, to behave in terms of reward and punishment. This is often the case when a child is overindulged materially but denied any deep personal love from her parents. Such a child soon learns that adherence to superficial acts of conformity and "model" behavior enables her to avoid punishment and often gain some positive attention in the form of rewards. However, since these can only partially satisfy one's needs for love, understanding and acceptance, such persons often are unable to develop the ability to enter into any truly deep interpersonal relationships. Instead, they establish a pattern of life which enables them to gain gratification of their desires with a minimum of "giving" on their part. The emotionally shallow personality which emerges fails to incorporate abstract values such as honesty, personal loyalty to others, or responsibility for personal actions.

It appears that Ann is this type of individual. She apparently felt that any behavior was alright in school as long as she avoided punishment. She conformed to her parents' expectations, (i.e. church attendance, regular school attendance, social values of honesty, etc.) without any emotional involvement as long as such behavior served a purpose for her (avoided punishment). Similarly, she regularly called her probation officer each day, but then she felt free to do as she pleased as soon as she had completed the call. This sneaky type of behavior reflects her basic lack of respect for other people and a learned pattern of social interaction involving manipulation to gain her own ends.

Ann stopped conforming when it became inconvenient in terms of her relationships with her peers. As needs for peer acceptance became more intense in early adolescence, she was able to shift her behavior patterns with no guilt. Since her only rationale for adherence to socially acceptable values was convenience, it was easy to adopt dissocial behavior when it served a more pressing purpose. While she lost the material rewards from her mother (in money, etc), she apparently gained enough in psychological rewards to make the sacrifice of the former worthwhile. Consequently, the immediate gratification of needs served as the prime motivator of her behavior.

Unfortunately, it is unlikely that Ann's behavior will be greatly changed by her experience of confinement. She appears to have a deeply ingrained pattern of behavior and she, no doubt, will continue to manipulate in her relationships. There is little indication that she is capable of any deeper relationships and it is unlikely that she'll develop the ability to sincerely care about anyone else or the total society. It is possible that she'll become more skillful in manipulation and more adept at avoiding being caught in her delinquent acts, or she may learn to manipulate within socially acceptable limits (i.e. cheat on income tax, use other people, etc.) if the results of her delinquent behavior involve too small a reward and too great a punishment. In either case, the resulting behavior will always reflect a weighing of these two variables in her mind in an attempt to gain her own selfish desires.

Patty L.

I first started getting into trouble with the police when I was twelve or thirteen years old. My brother and I were crazy about horses. The people that lived behind us owned some horses, so we always hung around there. We finally met this boy who was boarding his horse there. He talked real big. My brother and I thought he was really something, so we followed him and did what he suggested. One day he was shooting my brother's BB gun and we ran into this kid that he didn't like. So he started shooting this kid with the gun and then he forced him to smoke some cigarettes. This kid told his parents what happened and they called the police. The police talked to our friend and found out mine and my brother's names. They came over to my house and they put all the blame on us instead of the other guy. And this got our parents pretty mad at us, 'Course they took the police word for it. This got my brother and me mad and he started hating the police and breaking laws just to spite them.

After that we kept hanging around with kids that always got in trouble. We did bad things because I guess we were scared to be called "chicken." It's hard to be called "chicken" by our friends. I went around thinking I was something real great because I had a police record and no girls would dare to fight me 'cause they were scared of me. But I've always had some decent friends who were never in police trouble and they talked to me and kept me going pretty straight.

My family moved around a lot too, 'cause my dad thought if I got away from the crowd I was going with, everything would be okay. So we moved from our house in DuPage to Chicago. My brother and I were told not to come into DuPage anymore. But since my parents owned a home in the town, we thought we could go there anyway and not get in trouble. So one night we had a drinking party in our old home, since it was empty, and the police raided it. We were taken to court and placed on probation. My probation officer wanted me put away though, so my dad sent me to live with my aunt. After I was there for awhile I realized how much I loved my parents and how much I had hurt them by getting into trouble, so I begged my father to get me home. But my probation officer didn't want me to come back home, so my father moved out of state to Michigan, then I came home.

When summer was over, I started school. I got along real good with all the kids, but I didn't get along with the dean or my gym teacher. I ditched a half a day of school and the dean kicked me out of school for it and he also took me to court. But my dad wanted a lawyer so I got a thirty day continuance. During this time I was under house arrest but I left the house anyway. I was standing on the sidewalk by the school when my gym teacher walked by. Later that day, I got picked up and taken to a detention home until I went to court because the gym teacher had said I pushed her into a snowdrift. While I was in detention home my parents moved to Chicago because it was hard for my Dad to drive back and forth from Michigan to Chicago to go to work. When I went to court, the judge let me go home while I lived in

Chicago. I didn't ever get into trouble. Finally, my Dad decided to move back to DuPage, because he was getting kind of sickly and it didn't make any sense that he should have to pay rent for an apartment when we owned our own home. So we moved to Du-Page again. I got picked up by the police once for loitering, but my probation didn't do anything about it.

Now, I come to the reason I am here. All this time, since I was fourteen years old, I had been on probation for that drinking party. Now I am going on seventeen. Anyway, there was this girl that was going around town saying things about me. And they were pretty dirty. So I found her and I punched her two times, then I let her go. Her mother called the police on me. So my probation officer brought me into court and they sent me here to Geneva for violation of probation. And I didn't think this was too fair. I had been on probation for two and one-half years straight, even when I lived out of state I was still on probation in DuPage County. And my probation officer has always wanted me put away ever since she had charge of me.

But even though I've only been here almost a month and a half now, I think Geneva has really done a lot of good for me. I've had plenty of time to think and now I see my mistakes and where I have gone wrong. I know I will be a much better person when I get out of here because I love my parents very much, and I have hurt them too much already. I don't want to hurt them anymore because they have always been good to me and they don't deserve all the hurt I've given them. So just thinking about how much I love and miss them will be enough to keep me close to them and out of trouble for the rest of my life.

Patty appears to be a girl with little impulse control whose first difficulties occurred at early adolescence when she wanted to be a "big shot." Unsure of how to go about this, she was easily impressed by a boy who seemed to possess the confidence she lacked. When she and her brother were blamed for the other boy's misbehavior, rather than reject him they got angry at the police and their parents for believing them to be at fault. She then followed her brother's pattern of breaking laws to spite the police.

Her reaction of anger probably resulted from the expectation that her parents would defend her. It appears, throughout her story, that her father generally made all of the adjustments, accepting her impulsive acts and placing the blame on others. A child indulged in this way by an overpermissive parent does not gain self-control. Instead, she seems to believe he will always take care of the consequences of her actions.

Whenever she got in trouble, the family moved to "get her away from the crowd" who were a bad influence on her. When she was arrested for attending a drinking party in a town from which she'd been asked to leave, her father sent her to her aunt to prevent her being committed. When she wanted to return and her probation officer was against it, the father moved to another state so that she could have her way. In each instance she was able to manipulate the father so that she never had to suffer the consequences of her acts. Therefore, she had no need to learn self-control or responsibility.

It is not surprising that Patty disliked her probation officer and felt his recommended commitment to be unjust. Since she is accustomed to having her way, she strongly resents an authority figure who demands that she act more maturely or pay for her immaturity. Her behavior toward her teachers in school and impulsive fighting with other girls when she is dissatisfied with them reveals that she has not learned to respect any adult or the rights of others, as she has never had to do this in her own home.

While Patty expresses great remorse and repentance while she's confined, it is unlikely that her future behavior will be much different. Once she is again placed in the permissive environment of her home, she probably will revert to her old feelings and attitudes. It is unlikely that she will ever change unless the attitudes and behavior of her parents change and, even then, she probably would just resent them as she does other authority figures.

Betty R.

As far back as I remember was when I was three years old. I was outside jumping rope and I was told by my grandmother to put my shoes on. I took them off again and ran outside with them off.

I continued jumping rope and jumped on a bottle and cut my foot three different places. I was rushed to the doctor and bandaged up real fancy to mine eyes. I had to continue getting treatment for approximately seven months. All that time it gave me really a chance to get all the love and affection I needed by every member of the immediate family. I was always petted by my father and should have more love for him than any other. I loved my father, oh, so much! My father spent much more time and money on me than any other member of the family. He thought it fair because I loved him more and took in all the advice he gave. In my little world he was something like a god to me.

Then something tragic happen in my sight and dad's. My grandmother (his mother) died. It was in 1959. I was so afraid that not even my father couldn't soothe my hurting inside. He cried too, but I think if I collected all the tears I sheded, it would have been a river. After that I continue my moral life and oh I tried to give more love and affection to my father than before because that hurt lasted all his life. The good times I spent with my grandmother are still remembered. My life and his shaped up a little. To me, he was just realizing his mother was gone.

My problems began to build up and I began to talk more to my father. He took ill one day in 1962 and was rushed from work to the hospital. There, I was told he was in serious condition and I began to realize then that my father was dying. My mother is the strict type and means well. I starting doing mostly what she commanded because my father always told me, "As sick as I am, I may be dying soon, and when I leave I want you to obey your mother. That's the only thing I really want you to do." His words cling to me to this day, and I really would have disappointed him if he know all I did.

Soon after that I was told that he had a stroke. I was sure he was gone with this incident. God never heard me so much! However, he came through beautifully, but it really took time. I thanked God for all He had done. Myself — nothing cared to me just as long as I had my father. My life toward my father increased.

I began to gradually bring my mother in the picture. She

loved me also and because of her great love for my father it brought all us together. The date is not in my mind tho, but I remember having a bad tooth. I stayed home from school several days and finally my mother said "Betty, do you think you feel up to seeing a dentist?" I responded, saying "Yes." My mother didn't have time so my father took me to the dentist' office. He said it had to come out. My father said, "Don't cry," and he held my hand. It hurt, but I hardly didn't feel it because my father held my hand and I was still crying. When the dentist had finished, he took the pains from around me and I ran and hugged my father. My sister laughed at me (except of her to laugh to know I was suffering so much, she really has a heart).

Then my father took ill unexpectedly in December, 1964, and died. At that time, all I remember was my father gasping for breath. My mother and sister were running around crying there, and in trying to comfort my sister, my mother let my father die. I rid in the closet and began to cry and pray, but God didn't hear me. All I could remember was the good things we shared together — the dentist office, the death of my grandmother — just everything him and I enjoyed; I, with all my heart.

After the death of my father, I started going my way and got into more trouble in these two years than in the whole fourteen years of my life. I began to curse in everything I said. I began to stay up late. Everything anyone told me came in one ear and went out the other. I began to worry about the past, present and future. I became very upset and by me not trying to keep up any good health, I became weak and sick and had appointments to see all kind of doctors. I wouldn't eat unless my father was there and wouldn't sleep unless I knew that he was safe no matter where he was, just as long as heaven accepted him.

Between 1959 and 1966 I was exposed to tuberculosis. My aunt died from it and my uncle's case is under control. I had a couple of treatments and many x-rays and pills to take. The doctor said, "Keep warm and prevent cold." I tell you I had a cold every week and still gets them.

My first time at a police station was last year. My sister got out of hand and because of that my mother thought she would do better by sending her to Audy Home. I told her that if you take her, you have to take me; so both of us went. The commission talked to us and said, "Go home and straighten up." This most recent time was because they said I was involved in damaging of school property. I didn't do anything. They said I was involved in a lot of things, but all that they said isn't true. I suffered a lot for those things. My P.O. thought it might be good for us to come out to Geneva. I wasn't upset because I had enough problems. I really was more afraid if I took it too serious, I might have a nervous breakdown. So I accepted commitment here. After I told my sister, "Don't worry, we will at least be together and be good so we can see the beauty in our own home. It took awhile for her to accept, but she came through nicely. I get to visit her and discuss our further goal. It will be nice, when we go home because my mother said, "I'm praying for you girls and I know through God you'll come home alright." And these words I think of every time I think about getting in trouble; I take out the letter my family writes and just praise them for getting around to think about me after I had neglected them so much.

Here again, in Betty's story, we have the picture of an over-indulged child who clearly recognized that she was her father's favorite. Her earliest recollections involve an extended period of attention and affection received in connection with an injury resulting from not minding her grandmother. It is also interesting to note that her initial attachments involved her father and his mother rather than any closeness to her own mother, who apparently was also in the home. It seems feasible to assume that the mother did not fulfill the role of a mother in the eyes of this girl. Consequently, she apparently did not undergo the oedipal conflict, as the mother was ignored rather than viewed as a competitor.

Upon the death of the grandmother, this child, at age seven, felt that she should replace her grandmother in her father's life. Since the father encouraged and perpetuated her fantasy by over-indulgence and special attention, she began to believe that this should be expected simply because she cared so much. This relationship increased her dependency needs and her expectation that others should also be primarily concerned with her needs.

The loss of her father, who was her primary source of narcissistic supplies, was almost overwhelming. Aside from blaming her mother and sister for his death, she also strongly resented the fact that they were preoccupied with their loss and did not attempt to understand and give her sympathy during her period of despair and aloneness.

When they did not or were not able to meet her needs as her father had, she became quite bitter and rebelled against her mother's authority. Betty does not describe her offenses, so its difficult to know just what form this rebellion took other than disobeying and cursing. It does not appear, however, that she had a delinquent orientation. Her behavior seems largely an emotional reaction to her loss of a love object. Her story suggests a general depression and difficulty in interpersonal relationships, as she apparently did not find someone else to satisfy her now frustrated needs for love and attention.

It appears that, in response to the stress accompanying this period, she regressed to a less mature level as she once more sought this attention through illness. Since her injury at age three had brought love from everyone in the family, she now stopped eating until her health became very poor. The many appointments with doctors apparently, in part, showed her that someone cared about her.

It is suspected that Betty felt that her mother had rejected her as a child in preference for her sister. This, in part, would explain why she had formed such a strong attachment to her father. This also would explain her sarcastic remarks in relation to her sister, reflecting strong sibling rivalry. However, when Betty lost her father and was unable to gain gratification for her needs of acceptance and love to a sufficient degree through illness, she repressed her hostility toward her sister. Her need to be needed was apparently so great that she substituted her sister as her love object, becoming her protector and advocate, even offering to go to the Audy Home with her.

While Betty's sister, apparently, partially fulfills her needs, Betty still seems to feel that people accuse her unjustly, do not think of her and her feelings and cause her great suffering. She is still preoccupied with her insatiable dependency needs for love, belonging and attention. Unfortunately, it is not likely that she will ever find anyone who can give her as much as her needs demand. She will probably continue to seek some source of gratification, but will, likely, never overcome her basic feelings of rejection.

Ruth V.

I am an average girl of 16 with average family problems. My mother died when I was 12, and ever since then I've had nobody to turn to. I felt alone and unwanted. I had nobody who cared. At least that's what I thought. Then I ran away from home and got sent to Audy. I really felt let down then. But I wrote a letter to my father promising to do better if he would let me come home. So he took me home. I stayed for awhile and tried to do good. But it didn't last. I left home again, with my cousin, and we went out on the road. We met up with some dudes and lived with them for a few days. That is when I lost my virginity. At the age of 13. I didn't care of nobody else did. So I got busted and sent back to Audy. Then after 3½ months I was released and sent to a foster home in not too far away from my own home. I stayed there 2 weeks and ran again. I was sent to another foster home which I loved. It was only a temporary home so I ran again. I was living with my boyfriend for about 3 weeks, I got busted for curfew and the police found out I was on the run and sent me back to Audy. After staying 4 months there. I was sent to another foster home in Naperville. I stayed there about a month and ran. I got busted and sent back to Audy. I was there 1 week and got sent out here to ISTSG & BA. It was a real scary experience at first when I came. Then after I was here for awhile it didn't seem to be so bad. Then my cousin who works out in found out I was here and talked to his father and mother mother-in-law and asked them if they would take me so they did. And after 4 months here I went to their home in. I was there 2 months and messed up! I was sent back here for 9 months and I am going to a foster home on parole. It is in. I will do my best to make it this time cause' I'm tired of running and I want a home I can call my own. So

I'll give this home a fair chance. Not run like I did from the others. I hope I can make it this time! I'm going to finish high school and continue work in Beauty Culture. I hope I never see the inside of any kind of institution again!! I'm really gonna try and make it the best I possibly can.

Virginia C.

I was born in ———. When I was six I got adopted and when I was adopted I was always wishing I never was. When I was twelve years old my father left home. When I first got in trouble was with this girl that lived a block away. We would always be stealing and then since my father left my mother worked nights and I had parties all the time. Then the guys and chicks that use to come over would bring dope so I finally started with reefers. When the reefer didn't get me high anymore I started on acid. So then I got to the point where I didn't come home at night and didn't go to school. And when I did come home my mother who is a nurse and knew when I was high. I was in and out the Audy home five times. The last time I went to the Audy home was Dec. 29, 1972. When they released me they sent me to the shelter. And then I ran away from there. I was staying all over. I sometimes would just be walking the streets and staying at friends or brothers.

Then I started on harder dop snorting THC. My brother was married and told me to not do dope with him. Then one night I went to his house and I had a bag of "rifer". He told me to get rid of it so I went to the Pool hall and tried to sell it when a police man walked in. He told me I had a warrant out for my arrest and I still had the dope on me. They found the dope and I was charged with possession (truancy, runaway, curfew and violation of probation). Now since then I've been locked up for 6½ months.

Conclusions

In these few examples of probation violators, we find three girls unable to respond to a probation situation because each was basically incapable of forming a mature interpersonal relationship involving responsibility and concern on the part of both individuals. In each case, the girls' own needs were paramount. In the case of Ann, the probation officer was seen as someone to be used as a means to an end; Betty, preoccupied with her insatiable needs, disregarded her probation officer because she could not fulfill these needs; and Patty resented hers because she represented an obstacle, since she would not condone Patty's immature, self-centered behavior.

Consequently, regardless of how understanding and dedicated the probation officers attempted to be, they were not able to provide a relationship which could bring about behavioral changes. Apparently, the particular personality of the girl involved has a great effect upon the degree of success which can be obtained through a probation service.

REFERENCES

1. Newman, Charles L.: *Sourcebook on Probation, Parole and Pardons.* Springfield, Thomas, 1958, pp. 60, 69.
2. Reinemann, John Otto: Probation and the juvenile delinquent. *The Annals of The American Academy of Political and Social Science, 216*:109-119, January 1949.
3. Teeters, Negley K., and Reinemann, John Otto: *The Challenge of Delinquency.* New York, P-H, 1950, pp. 384-385.
4. Chute, Charles Lionel, and Bell, Marjorie: *Crime, Courts and Probation.* New York, Macmillan, 1956, p. 136.
5. Crystal, David: Family casework in probation. *Federal Probation, XIII*:47-53, December 1949.
6. Johnson, Arne R.: Recent developments in the law of probation. *J Criminal Law, Criminology and Police Science, 53*:201, June 1962.
7. Cavan, Ruth S.: *Juvenile Delinquency.* Philadelphia, Lippincott, 1962, p. 287.
8. Hardman, Dale G.: The function of the probation officer. *Federal Probation, 24*:4, September 1960.
9. England, Ralph W., Jr.: What is responsible for satisfactory probation and post-probation outcome? *J Criminal Law, Criminology and Police Science, 47*:667-677, March-April, 1957.
10. Kay, Barbara A., and Vedder, Clyde B.: *Probation and Parole.* Springfield, Thomas, 1963, p. 92.

CHAPTER 8

THE TRUANT GIRL

W HILE THE HOME IS THE FIRST and most important influence in shaping the personality and character of the child, other environmental forces, such as the school, also help to determine them. The school is perhaps the most important community agency involved in the effort to prevent delinquency, since it reaches practically all children at a relatively early period of their growth.

Children who are frustrated in school and become delinquent show consistent records of truancy, retardation and marked antipathy toward school. The reasons for such strong antipathy include the inability to learn, resentment of restriction and routine and lack of interest, in that order. Delinquents seem to show a distaste for subject matter which demands strict logical reasoning, persistency of effort and good memory, such as is required in arithmetic, social studies, foreign languages, science and commercial subjects. Block and Flynn conclude that the school contributes to delinquency by accentuating delinquent trends in children who are already predelinquent, actively delinquent or emotionally disturbed. Both the school and the juvenile court recognize the fact that delinquency frequently can be prevented by redirecting the child's antisocial and destructive impulses.[1]

For many maladjusted and potentially delinquent children, school seems to be just another frustrating and unhappy experience. The school may intensify feelings of frustration and inadequacy generated in the family and play groups. Many pupils caught in this cycle seek an outlet for their frustrations in truancy and delinquent behavior. Truancy has been called the "kinder-

garten of crime," for often the young truant, under the influence
of older boys and girls, learns techniques of forbidden activities
during the stolen hours. The frequency of truancy and dishonesty
noted in school children before their first contact with the law,
suggests that an efficient visiting teacher or counselor program
might have prevented some later delinquencies.[2]

In the study of Sidney Axelrad's Negro and white male
institutionalized delinquents, it was found that white delinquents
were more prone to be committed for truancy than the Negro
delinquents; 38 per cent as opposed to 18 per cent. This should
not be understood to mean that the white children were more
poorly adjusted than the Negro children — almost all the delinquents had school problems — it is rather that the community,
or at least the school system, considers truancy in the white child
as something about which it is willing to take positive action.
Seemingly, it does not care as much in the case of the Negro
child.[3]

The magnitude of the nonattendance problem is worthy of
serious consideration. In urban areas of the United States, roughly
12 per cent of all pupils are absent from school on any given day.
Most nonattendance is not truancy, however. Only about 13 per
cent of all school absences have nonmedical causes, according to
Alfred J. Kahn.[4]

Kahn distinguishes between various categories of children not
attending school. The "lawful absentee" is the child whose excuse
is acceptable according to the criteria of a given school system.
The "unlawful absentee' is the child without any explanation, or
the child whose explanation is unacceptable. The "truant" is the
juvenile who has been absent without the knowledge or permission of the parents. It is a fair estimate that not over 15 per
cent, and probably closer to 10 per cent, of all school absentees
represent truancy.

Kahn summarizes the major considerations for those in child-
helping services as follows: (a) many truants never become serious
delinquents, (b) more truants than nontruants are potential
delinquents, (c) the major importance of truancy is that it identifies a child who may be in trouble.

Whether it is termed "lawful absence," "unlawful absence" or "truancy," the fact remains that both delinquent and non-delinquent girls indulge themselves in this activity. In the study of delinquent behavior in high school and correctional school girls, Short and Nye noted that 41 per cent of the high school girls and 94 per cent of the correctional school girls had "skipped school." Of the high school girl group, 12.2 per cent admitted skipping school more than once or twice and 66.3 per cent of the correctional school girls admitted skipping school more than once or twice.[5]

According to John Otto Reinemann, in practically all juvenile court laws the term "delinquency" is defined so as to indicate truancy, thus establishing the jurisdiction of the juvenile court in such cases. Any effective program of controlling truancy demands a close cooperation between the board of education and the juvenile court, and a clear understanding of the limits of their respective functions.[6]

As John R. Ellingston points out, the defiance of law and authority involved in truancy usually means that the child has reached a major crisis in her life. Probably the school — perhaps the family, the home or the community — has become intolerable, and she runs away from it. This calls not for strong-armed attendance officers, nicknamed "talent scouts for the reform schools," but for teachers trained in casework.[7]

In a more recent study of truancy in San Francisco, as quoted by Cavan, the median I.Q. for truants was 95, with a range from 43 to 163, compared with a median of approximately 100 for all students. Truants were poorly adjusted academically, with 70 per cent retarded at least one semester. In 70 per cent of the truancy cases, such difficulties as illness, running away, stealing, nervousness, deviant sex acts and fighting were noted. In 50 per cent of the cases, situational factors were prominent, such as lack of clothing, school too difficult or child not accepted by other pupils. In 30 per cent of the cases, the pupil was withdrawn, depressed, ill or daydreamy. In 20 per cent of the cases, the pupil was aggressive and apparently had truanted to get even with the world. The high percentage of truants found among delinquents seems to indicate a tendency of the boy or girl not to adapt to an orderly way of life.[8]

Truancy is clearly associated with later criminal records in both male and female. Of the recidivists reentering prison, at least three-fourths have truancy listed on their records. Even those entering prison for the first time, the majority, over 60 per cent, on their own admission will recall being off-the-record truants. This is a serious indictment of our schools. The public school becomes such an anathema to some juvenile delinquents that they fail to realize that a reformatory is basically a school.

The following case history illustrates one girl's attempt to "fight back" against the overwhelming demands of her father and her successive failures in school, by resorting to truancy and delinquent acts.

Faye M.

Faye is a fifteen-year-old white girl who was committed to a state training school for truancy. Approximately one year prior to her commitment, she first came to the attention of the juvenile court for running away from home. During the time that she was absent from the home, she reputedly stayed with a married man and frequented night clubs. Her record reveals that on several occasions following that, she again left home, staying with girlfriends overnight or sleeping in the park. A number of times she was found wandering the streets.

She truanted frequently and on one occasion became involved in a burglary with another girl and several older boys. She was also picked up for shoplifting, with other boys and girls who had juvenile records. Finally, the junior high school which she attended refused to accept her back.

Faye is the youngest of four children, two of whom are married and no longer living in the home. The family lives in a middle-income neighborhood and the parents own the house. The home is described as a modern house with modern conveniences but old furnishings. Faye has her own room.

Although the father has only completed the eighth grade, he has been employed regularly by a manufacturing company. He is described as a very rigid and controlling person. Faye attributes her behavior to the unreasonable demands of her father.

The mother, in contrast, is somewhat quiet, lackadaisical and depressed. She complains of several minor physical ailments as well as menopausal symptoms. She, also, has had a limited education; she completed the ninth grade. She has never worked outside the home. Both parents were in their late forties at the time of Faye's commitment.

Faye's school records revealed that she disliked school and was in continual conflict with the school authorities. Furthermore, the officials believed that she was of borderline intelligence and unable to function successfully in her normal grade placement. They felt her truancy resulted from this handicap and recommended that she be placed in a class for the educable mentally handicapped.

However, at the training school she was tested and found to possess greater intellectual functioning than previously thought. She made fairly satisfactory adjustments in the normal classroom setting there.

During her stay, her parents visited frequently and a better relationship was established between Faye and her father. When she was paroled to her home after six months, the parents entered counseling class to learn more appropriate ways of working with their daughter. Faye returned to a school program which consisted of half-time academics and half-time occupational crafts such as sewing and cooking, which she enjoyed very much.

In this case, we see a girl who believed she was incapable of meeting the demands of her father. Apparently, the mother gave her little support and she felt quite inadequate and frustrated in the home setting.

Faye found no greater success in school. She seemed to have difficulty in dealing with all authority figures. This could reflect an attitude of futility, since she had a background of failure in her relationships with authority at home. It could also reflect some displacement of the anger and frustration which she felt toward her father's unreasonable demands. Further complicating the situation was the fact that the school officials regarded her as intellectually incapable of success. No doubt their recommendation that she be placed in a special class further decreased her motivation to attend school and increased her feelings of inadequacy.

It does appear, however, that Faye was somewhat retarded academically, since she apparently was not keeping up with her class. Whether this resulted from truancy, inattention, lack of motivation or intellectual limitations, is unclear. However, it appears that little was done by the school to help her work through her problems or to encourage her to utilize the potential which she possessed.

Since she had experienced relatively little success in either setting, it is not surprising that she attempted to escape both frustrating situations whenever possible. Her involvement in delinquent acts probably resulted from her need to gain acceptance somewhere, as it appears that she usually followed the lead of other youths who had delinquent histories. Faye, like many insecure adolescents, no doubt felt further rejection by her family, and even society as a whole, was not too great a price to pay for at least a temporary sense of belonging.

Occasionally, truant behavior occurs because the parents do not value education and the child develops this pattern with their encouragement. The following case history reveals such a situation.

Edith C.

Edith is a fifteen-year-old white girl whose school records revealed irregular attendance dating from the time she entered first grade at eight years of age. It was reported that her mother did not want her to attend school at all. Edith was kept at home where the mother would hold and rock her because she supposedly was ill. However, the doctor's report revealed that Edith was in good health.

When her truancy continued, several investigations were made of the home situation by the truant officer. Each time Edith refused to go to school, and subsequent interviews with the mother revealed that she had usually given Edith permission to remain at home.

At the court hearing regarding this persistent truant behavior, the mother admitted that she could not control her daughter. Community efforts then were sought to help Edith, but both she and her mother rejected all attempts. For example, when Edith told the truant officer that she couldn't go to school because of a lack of clothing, the church obtained clothes for her. In response, Edith either gave them away or burned them, refusing to wear the clothes.

The church also made arrangements for her to go to the beauty shop to help improve her personal appearance. However, Edith would not go unless the truant officer escorted her there and remained the entire time with her. The mother apparently lent little support to any of these efforts. Instead, she seemed to try to perpetuate Edith's immaturity and to keep her from growing up.

When Edith reached early adolescence, she turned to relatives to gain some understanding of the numerous physical changes she was undergoing. However, the mother threatened to call the police, as she felt that Edith might become pregnant if she had greater knowledge about sex.

The mother did not become greatly concerned about her until Edith began to spend a great deal of time with a thirty-year-old cousin, whom she considered to be a bad influence on Edith. As she began to remain away from home a great deal, the mother became fearful that she was beginning to follow the pattern of an older sister who had been difficult to control and who had become illegitimately pregnant. Therefore, the mother requested that Edith be sent to the training school. She appeared relieved that Edith was committed, as she felt incapable of coping with her and there were no other older relatives to provide adequate supervision.

Edith was the seventh of eight children born to parents in very poor circumstances. Their only source of income was through public assistance. The father, age seventy-nine, was twenty years older than the mother and was considered to be senile. He also had a physical handicap. Further limiting his ability to provide for his children was the fact that he had had no formal education and was completely illiterate.

The mother had had a fifth grade education. In addition to being mentally retarded, she was in poor physical and mental health, having been a voluntary patient on several occasions at the state mental hospital. This marriage was her third and the father's first. She reported that her first marriage was of only three month's duration and that no children were born of that union. She remarried two years later but separated soon afterwards. The six older children of her present marriage are much older than Edith, ranging in age from twenty to forty-five years.

The neighborhood in which the family lived has been described as one having a high delinquency rate (two of Edith's older brothers, ages 20 and 23, as well as her younger brother, 13, have been involved in delinquent behavior). Most of the homes in the area are deteriorated and most of the residents are receiving public assistance.

At the girl's training school, Edith was described as being a very deficient, rustic girl who projected and denied any responsibility for her behavior. She was found to be functioning in the dull-normal range of intelligence. She was very timid and withdrawn, reacting with much anxiety toward authority figures as well as toward her peers.

In counseling, she revealed that she was dependently tied to her mother, feeling that her father had completely rejected her because he had often hit her. The extremely overprotective irresponsible behavior of her mother had apparently made adjustments in the home most difficult to her.

Edith was placed in a full day-school program in which she worked very hard, adjusting well to the classroom situation. Although she initially had difficulty establishing relationships with the other girls, in time, with help, she was able to make a better adjustment.

Because of the unfavorable home situation and the limitations of her parents, a foster-home group placement was arranged. Edith was placed in the foster home after six months at the training school. Reports during her parole period suggested that she was making a very good adjustment with an experienced foster mother.

This is a case of an intellectually limited girl responding to her environment. Both parents, apparently, were physically and mentally incapable of caring for her. In such a culturally deprived atmosphere, she was so limited in experience as well as direction that she failed to learn to utilize what ability she possessed.

Mentally retarded individuals need consistent instruction and guidance so that they can learn their strengths and limitations. In Edith's case, however, her mother attempted to protect her by restricting her interaction with others. Whereas she might have gained some skills in school, her mother's attempts to keep her at home only served to encourage her to avoid school and other people. As a result, she did not gain any social skills and became more dependent upon her mother.

It is difficult to ascertain how much of Edith's low intellectual functioning reflects physical limitations and how much of it results from her deprived background. However, mental retardates usually respond well to environmental changes, as they utilize conformity as a means to cope and as a defense. Therefore, it is quite likely that Edith will continue to do well in her present setting, and if she is placed in a school program geared to her capabilities, she probably could learn to become a productive, law-abiding citizen, provided she is given attention, guidance and sincere concern.

The following story, written by a girl commited for truancy, reveals her inability to cope with the dependency — independency conflict of adolescence.

Jane M.

Well, as far as I remember, I was about four years old and just getting ready for school, but I had to wait 'till I was five years old to start. I didn't want to start because I didn't want to go to first grade instead of kindergarten. But I was to go, I guess, on account of having been to a nursery school earlier, and my mother wanted me to be up with my cousin because we're the same age and she had started before me. After I started, I became very fond of school and wouldn't have missed it for no one. It was that way up until the seventh grade and just stopped all of a sudden.

At first I was going to start back and then my stepfather would tell me, "Why don't you go on like you are suppose to?" That just made me mad, so I wouldn't go back. Then as I just got tired of not having anything to do. I tried going back to school and it worked. So I just stayed in school awhile and then I started getting into trouble with girls in my room. So I asked my mother to get me a transfer and she said that I shouldn't get a transfer because it was almost passing time. Since they didn't have the next grade I was suppose to enter, I had to transfer anyway. So I just started keeping to myself and just a few friends because I felt that if I just didn't bother with the ones that didn't want my friendship, I'd be better off and so accomplish a little bit more.

When school started again in September and I was transferred, I even felt I had a better chance here, but I was mistaken. When my mother took me to school, which was customary with her, my classmates had a story about me, but I didn't know it. At the time they all seemed very nice except a very few. That didn't count much because they all were choosy about their friends. After I was there awhile I found I didn't get along with the teachers. Every time I asked to do a certain problem or to read when we have oral reading they wouldn't let me, so I decided I wasn't wanted or didn't belong there. So I stopped again and my mother encouraged me to go back again but I wasn't set on going back because I felt that it would only mean trouble with others. I didn't want that, only to be friends as only a person can.

And when I went back, everything was all right until my library teacher accused me of having several books, which I didn't have except for one, and she didn't even mention that one. So, naturally, I felt bad about it. I talked it over with my mother and she said maybe the teacher was mistaken, but I soon found out that she was going to suspend me from school and make me pay for the books. I told my mother and she told me to just take back the one I had. I did, but the teacher still suspended me from school. I told her I wasn't going to pay for them. When it came time to pass again, she held my report card and said I wasn't going without paying for those books. I got mad and asked for a transfer but the principal wouldn't give me one.

I just forgot about it and everything went all right for awhile.

Then one afternoon we were in homemaking class. A friend, well at least a suppose-to friend, let me wear her watch, and when I got ready to go home I said, "Here is your watch," and she told me to keep it for her until the next day. So I said, "Okay," and when I got home I told my mother about it. She told me to take it back to her, but at the time I didn't know where she lived and so she told me to take it back the next day. I was sick, so I didn't go to school the next day. I did go to school the following day. I was called to the office and they said I was accused of taking her watch, but she wasn't at school. I had let my brother wear her watch in case he saw her first, so when I saw her cousin, I asked her where did she live. She told me, and instead of going back to school, I went over to her house, but there wasn't no one at home and it was too late to go to school, so I didn't go back that day or the next. I decided, since she said I stole her watch, I was going to make it true.

After that, I just kept it and missed another day of school. My mother thought I was going to school until my truant officer asked my mother to come up to the school, and on the way they saw me on the way to school. I was late but still on the way, because I didn't feel right being out of school when my mother thought I was there. I didn't have the watch with me. My brother still had it because I had decided I wasn't exactly going to keep it after all but give it back to her eventually, but not as yet. But mother told me I had to give it back to her then. So I said I lost it. The truant officer asked me where it was and I said I didn't know. He told me if I didn't tell him and my mother where it was I was going get into some trouble. I told them that my brother had it, so he drove me and my mother to where my brother went. He got it and took it back to the girl and told my mother to bring me to school the next day. He said if I didn't come he was going to send me to Motley.

The next day my mother got ready to take me to school and I went, but when I got there I refused to go in my classroom. So my mother told me if I didn't she was going to take me to the office. I wouldn't, so she took me to the office. They said they would take me to Motley and I said I didn't care. The truant officer said he'd give me another chance and he'd help me all he could. I told him I didn't want his help because I didn't need it. He said he didn't think I really wanted to go and I said I didn't care. He said it wasn't what I wanted, it was what I was going to get. So it was decided that I go to Motley 'til I graduate. He drove me and my mother to the school where I was to go, and after that I went to school regularly for awhile until I stopped. I was sent to Parental, where I stayed six weeks, and was then released to mother's custody. I still didn't go to school, so they sent me here.

Now I see where all my mistakes were and why they were caused, and I feel that they were partly my fault. When I leave here, I am going to start all over and to better myself in every way possible and go to school and get an education, because that is what's really needed to perform a much happier life.

The conflicts which Jane encountered are not atypical; they represent the kinds of problems many girls who are fearful of growing up encounter. Unfortunately, she was not given sufficient support and guidance to help her through the transition period of early adolescence. So her behavior shifted radically back and forth from extremely dependent, conforming behavior to impulsive rebellion, as she attempted to find her own solution.

Apparently, Jane did not have a basically delinquent orientation; rather, it is suspected that throughout grade school she was a conforming "good" little girl who tried to please her teachers and her mother. She was happy and looked forward to each day in school. She probably received enough recognition and acceptance by adults that she was not concerned about learning interpersonal skills or about gaining acceptance from her peers.

It is not unusual to find girls who, upon entering school, transfer their dependency from their mother to the teacher. Such children constantly seek attention and recognition by enthusiastically participating in all classroom work, volunteering to read and generally trying to excel in the eyes of the teacher. They usually report regularly to their mothers all of the events which happen in school, as Jane did.

This type of behavior brings many rewards to a child at the elementary school level, as other children tend to admire the child who does well, even though they may at the same time resent some of her self-centered attention seeking. Other children are not aware that her behavior really reflects strong dependency needs and that this form of regular reward serves to let her know that she is "good" and, therefore, acceptable.

However, such a child usually encounters great difficulty when she approaches adolescence, because her age-mates then transfer their dependency from adults to peers. Their criteria for acceptability is then determined by the degree of popularity one has with other teenagers. Whereas, behavior before was modeled after the parents and teachers' expectations and values, it now must fulfill the expectations of friends.

Although Jane does not explain why she suddenly stopped going to school in the seventh grade, it is suspected that she was no longer achieving the kind of success and acceptance which she had previously known in school. Furthermore, although she continued in her previously learned patterns of conformity, her peers now rejected her because of this behavior. It is also quite likely that her teachers at the seventh-grade level attempted to discourage her strong dependency on them by failing to provide the kinds of rewards which she had learned to expect, because they realized her behavior, alienated her from her peers. In response, Jane tried to avoid the school situation, with which she could not cope, through truancy.

When a conflict like this begins to overwhelm individuals, they often try to revert to patterns of behavior which had been successful in the past. No doubt Jane attempted to transfer her dependency back to her parents. Her truancy from school, she hoped, would cause them enough concern that they would coax and encourage her to return, and their attention would substitute for the lost rewards in the school setting. However, instead, her stepfather just said, "Why don't you go on to school like you are supposed to?" In a sense, he was transferring the responsibility for her actions back to her; he would not reward her for being a "good" little girl. This angered Jane, and just as a small child rebels and has a temper tantrum when he cannot gain his own way, Jane rebelled and continued to skip school to spite him.

Such behavior, however, provided little satisfaction for her. She was bored with nothing to do, she felt guilty because she knew her mother thought she acted like a three-year-old and she now had no source of narcissistic supplies from which to gain a sense of acceptance and self-worth. Consequently, she again returned to school.

This time Jane tried to win approval from her girlfriends by getting into trouble with them. This, apparently, was not too satisfying either, as she experienced such guilt that she asked her mother to have her transferred to a new school.

Since her mother told her that she shouldn't transfer until the end of the year, as she would have to go to ninth grade at a new high school anyway, she decided to withdraw from those persons who didn't want her friendship and bide her time. She succeeded in this action because she believed that things would be different in the new school and she'd start off on a better footing there.

It is apparent that her mother, in part, perpetuated this immaturity, as Jane states that her mother took her to the new school on the first day. It is understandable why her new classmates talked about her, as few ninth-graders are this dependent. It is also not surprising that they did not welcome her with open arms into their cliques. Girls at this age are particularly critical of behavior which they view as "babyish."

Since she was unable to establish rapport with other girls her age, she attempted to utilize the behavior which she had used to gain the approval of teachers. When they did not call upon her or include her enough to satisfy her needs, she again felt unwanted and withdrew into truancy. Even though her mother encouraged her to return, she did so reluctantly because she still had not learned how to cope with this new situation and was too fearful to act independently, as her friends did, and too immature to accept any personal responsibility for learning more mature social skills.

When she came in conflict with the librarian and was accused of irresponsibility in connection with returning books, Jane was greatly offended that the librarian did not seem to trust and believe her. She immediately turned to her mother for guidance and simply complied with her suggestion to return the book. When this did not resolve the conflict, she again responded immaturely, insisting that she would not accept responsibility or pay for the lost books. Again she tried to escape through transfer, but being unsuccessful, she just remained in the situation until her next conflict.

It is suspected that Jane was rather casual about responsibilities in general, as she appeared to have several misunderstandings with others. In the case of the watch, she obviously viewed herself as the injured party because she felt that she'd attempted to do the right thing and that others were unfair to accuse her wrongly. In fact, however, she was ambivalent about returning it because of her anger over the original misunderstanding. Her rebellion in response only got her into more and more difficulty. At that time, she, no doubt, really wanted to prove her independence by rejecting the truant officer's offer of help. However, each time she tried to assert herself, she was unable to tolerate the consequences and eventually had to escape again by avoidance (truancy).

Many of Jane's difficulties could have been avoided through some realistic counseling and strong direction from someone who could have helped her to accept responsibility for her actions. Her fear of growing up impeded her growth and brought about rejection by her peers. It is suspected that Jane will still need a great deal of help before she will be able to cope, as she does not seem to have any insight into why she has been so unsuccessful in her interpersonal relationships in the past.

Conclusions

Truancy can occur for a number of reasons: intellectual limitations, successive academic failure, overwhelming parental demands, parental rejection, peer and teacher rejection, lack of social skills, immaturity and excessive dependency needs. In each case, regardless of the factors causing her tortured perception, the girl views the school situation as so frustrating, unsatisfactory and uncomfortable that she utilizes the immature defense of avoidance employed by the runaway. However, most truants appear to lack the degree of independence necessary to leave the home entirely for extended periods and, therefore, eventually vacillate between two fears—that of being with people who reject them and that of being completely alone. Although they utilize avoidance when the rejection becomes too great, they still constantly seek the situation or way in which they can ultimately gain acceptance.

If the schools could provide an atmosphere of total acceptance of all individuals, accompanied by consistent success experiences, and teach them the social skills necessary to gain peer approval, these girls would be in a position to learn better ways of coping with and accepting the inevitable frustrations of life.

REFERENCES

1. Bloch, Herbert A., and Flynn, Frank T.: *Delinquency: The Juvenile Offender in America Today.* New York, Random, 1956, pp. 198-202.
2. Vedder, Clyde B.: *Juvenile Offenders.* Springfield, Thomas, 1963, pp. 58-60.
3. Axelrad, Sidney: Negro and white male institutionalized delinquents. *A J Sociology, VVII*:569-574, May 1952.
4. Kahn, Alfred J.: Who are our truants? *Federal Probation, XV*:35-50, March 1951.
5. Short, James F., Jr., and Nye, F. Ivan: Extent of unrecorded juvenile delinquency, tentative conclusions. *J Criminal Law, Criminology and Police Science, 49*:296-302, 1958.
6. Reinemann, John Otto: The truant before the court. *Federal Probation, XII*:8-12, September 1948.
7. Ellingston, John R.: *Protecting Our Children From Criminal Careers.* New York, P-H, 1948, pp. 285, 290.
8. Cavan, Ruth Shonle: *Juvenile Delinquency.* Philadelphia, Lippincott, 1962, p. 187.

CHAPTER 9

OBSERVATIONS, CONCLUSIONS AND RECOMMENDATIONS

T HE AUTHORS HAVE NOTED THE LACK of consensus and precise- ness in the definition of terms describing the offenses which lead to commitment. While the anticipated variation of recorded offenses among states and the fluctuations of offenses from year to year within states were observed, nevertheless offenses dubbed the "big five" appeared most consistently. These are (1) running away, (2) incorrigibility, (3) sexual offenses, (4) probation viola- tion and (5) truancy, often in that order. Approximately 75 to 85 per cent of the offenses leading to commitment of delinquent girls are found in the "big five" grouping. The underlying vein of many of these offenses is sexual misconduct by the girl delin- quent. However, in most instances the most innocuous charges of "running away," "incorrigibility," "ungovernability" and the like are used on the official record. It is for this reason that sexual offenses are in third place.

This survey supports the fact that state training schools for girls have a population of individuals with divergent problems and backgrounds. Many schools have large populations and a very high percentage of black girls committed from large metropolitan areas. Whereas per capita cost is difficult to assess because of the variation in what is included, the survey does reveal the high cost of treating delinquents in institutions. It is believed that this cost could be reduced by greater use of community services and com- munity-based programs for delinquents as well as for predelin- quents.

The offenses leading to commitment, as defined by the courts, are limited to various types of delinquent actions and antisocial behavior. The training school or central agency is confronted with the necessity of making a thorough analysis of the factors which have contributed to the development of the antisocial behavior in order to plan an effective treatment and rehabilitation program directed toward the return of the girl to the community. In communities where the courts have clinical services, clinical reports are helpful to the schools or central agencies in gaining deeper insights into the dynamics of the problem. Refinements in clinical services of the courts and the availability of specialized services in all juvenile courts would be an invaluable resource in diagnostic evaluations and placement of children in accordance with their needs. Sharper focus on the gaps in available community resources would be revealed. The necessity for planning an action-coordinated community program for the needs of these children would contribute much to the prevention, treatment and control of juvenile delinquency and crime.

The impact of the work of the Division of Juvenile Delinquency Service of the Children's Bureau of the United States on Children and Youth, the enactment of the Juvenile Delinquency and Youth Offenses Control Act of 1961 and the Economic Opportunity Act of 1964, should all contribute manifold, far-reaching results in a broadly based, community-wide effort not only to prevent delinquency, but to improve services to the adjudicated delinquent. These programs should meet the challenge of reestablishing the delinquent girl and help all delinquents and their families in sharing the benefits of our affluent American society.

In Chicago, the program of the Correctional Services Division of the Joint Youth Development Committee of the Department of Human Resources, under the leadership of Miss Betty Begg and Dr. Denton Brooks, represents a gigantic step forward. This is exemplified by a coordinated effort of agencies in the juvenile correctional and law enforcement field to unite in an "all-out attack" on juvenile delinquency, a complex phenomenon that strikes at the basic foundations of our society.

In the cases presented, the importance of having knowledge and understanding of sociological, cultural, psychological and physical factors in the delinquent behavior of the girls is clearly demonstrated. The need for a thorough diagnostic evaluation, drawn from experts in the various disciplines, is essential to the planning of an effective treatment and rehabilitation program. The important role of the social workers, the psychologists, the psychiatrists, the educators, the chaplains, the cottage parents, the work supervisors and the parole officers is reflected in the cases presented. The courts, police, community agencies, schools and social agencies give evidence of the importance and the nature of these contacts with the girl and her family prior to the adjudication and commitment process.

The cases also clearly point out the importance of a broad, diversified institutional program to cope with the various areas of difficulty encountered by these girls. It is evident that some girls responded to the external controls and milieu of the institutional setting while others, whose problems were primarily psychological and internalized, responded to the individual professional services offered. The recognition that the needs of all committed delinquent girls cannot be met within the institution was exemplified in the case of the girl who received psychiatric care on an outpatient basis while in the community and under the supervision of the parole officer in the Field Services Division of the Illinois Department of Corrections. Greater emphasis should be placed on providing community-based treatment programs. The advantage of a central agency having authority to transfer a committed delinquent to a service suitable to the treatment needs and interests of the youngster is self-evident in this case.

Since all persons working in the institutions affect the rehabilitation of the delinquent to some degree, efforts should be made to coordinate all services so that consistent philosophy, attitudes and treatment are employed in working with each girl and her particular problem and needs. Since most offenses leading to commitment are usually the culmination of a series of difficulties which began at an early age and, in part, reflect some disturbance in the child's primary relationship with her parents, particular attention should be given to the selection and training of cottage parents. Living with a group of girls in a twenty-four-hour real-life situation, these persons must be able to cope with "all" of the various patterns of behavior which serve as releases for the girls' frustrations, hostilities and anxieties. It is, therefore, extremely important that each cottage parent has some understanding of psychodynamics and receives professional assistance in working with these girls.

Since most of the institutions have predominantly female personnel, serious consideration should be given to involving more males in the programs. Few girls seem to have had the experience of a positive relationship with an adult male. Such an experience could greatly increase their ability to cope with heterosexual social situations when they return to the community.

The various cases point up the frequency of the pattern of avoidance (truancy and runaway) and the related problems associated with leaving the structure of school and/or home, such as sexual offenses, drinking and other acts. This suggests the need for closer attention to the preventive aspects of delinquency through early detection and counseling in the community for the runaway girl. The significance and importance of community programs in the area of delinquency and prevention of juvenile delinquency and crime has been widely documented.

While the home is the first and most important influence in shaping the personality and character of the child, other community and environmental forces such as the school help to determine them also. It goes without saying that since the school reaches practically all children at a relatively early period of their growth and development, it is the most strategic community institution in efforts to prevent delinquency and to help in the rehabilitation of the delinquent child.

It is recognized that many problems which students, especially low-income students, bring into schools are not the primary responsibility of the schools. But they must be dealt with if effective learning is to occur. Although the school is in a strategic position to identify problems, it is not equipped to handle the underlying precipitating conditions. Therefore, the school must join other community agencies in a team effort to work on these problems.

The unique contribution that the school can make in the prevention of delinquency and crime should not be minimized. Students exhibiting symptoms of emotional problems and social maladjustment require special attention. Basic understanding of their background and cultural conditions and taking these into consideration in the educational program are of paramount importance. This is especially important for teachers from the middle and upper income backgrounds working in ghetto areas. The same principle certainly should apply to teachers working in affluent communities.

Of basic importance in any school program is the realization that the school is working with growing personalities who enter the classroom with attitudes and feelings already shaped by the home, the family and the neighborhood environment. Children come to school with likes and dislikes, fears and anxieties . . . unsatisfied cravings and unfulfilled desires and aspirations. Love, attention, recognition and acceptance are basic needs of all human beings.

If teachers fail to recognize and take into account cultural and social conditions and basic human needs in the educational process, some children will rebel against school, become hostile and resentful, feel rejected, and may then take the first step toward delinquency and crime. Documented research reveals that children who are frustrated in school and become delinquent show consistent records of truancy, retardation and antipathy toward school.

Schools and other community institutions should involve youths in participating in planning and facilitating communication between adults. Involvement and participation by indigenous groups and local community persons is an approach utilized over thirty years ago by Clifford Shaw in the prevention of juvenile delinquencies. Today, high priority is given in the various experimental federal programs to involving those individuals in the community concerned with the identification and solution of social problems affecting them.

The Center for Inner-City Studies of Northeastern Illinois State College and other public and private colleges and universities are providing special training for student-teachers and experienced teachers in preparing them for teaching in inner-city schools. Courses in juvenile delinquency and criminology should be a requirement. House Bill No. 1407, the mandatory special education program established in the 1965 session of the federal legislature, should have a strong impact in dealing with socially maladjusted and emotionally disturbed children.

A comprehensive community program to reduce, to control and to prevent juvenile delinquency is as much the responsibility of the school as it is of those directly concerned with this ever increasing insidious problem which strikes at the very core of our society. To fail our children and youth in the education of the "whole" person in the full attainment of meaningful education in preparation for constructive and productive living is an indictment against each responsible member of the community.

The Church, the oldest and most established institution in the community, should play a dynamic role in the prevention of delinquency and crime. In fulfilling its primary responsibility for spiritual guidance, the Church (or Synagogue) should help the child develop regard for other persons and respect for their rights. In developing positive values, the Church and Synagogue can help the child to gain a perspective of life that will make him able to distinguish between sound fundamental values and transient ideas regarding the constitution of acceptable and unacceptable behavior. Hopefully, through the inculcation of these positive values, supported by home and school training, children will be enabled to face difficulties and gain understanding of the ultimate meaning of life. Thus they should be fortified against delinquency.

The Church and Synagogue should afford a place and an opportunity for young people to form wholesome associations and to participate in constructive activities. Serving as a community center in which boys and girls as well as entire families and neighbors may join such activities as clubs, discussion groups, choirs, recreation, spiritual guidance by private counseling, religious instruction and special programs can have a meaningful influence in the community. Special attention should be given to preparation for marriage. The Cana-Conference, sponsored by the Chicago Catholic Archdiocese, and other similar groups have made a tremendous contribution in this area. Harvey L. Long, former Executive Secretary of the Illinois Youth Commission, poses a most relevant question: "Is it not the mission of the Church to help maintain competent community services, be they police or other, and set good examples of honest, sincere, law-abiding adults as models for youth?".[1]

The authors recommend that organized recreational and leisure-time organizations critically examine their programs in meeting the needs of youth. Although it is recognized that wholesome activities offer children a channel for constructive and satisfying experience and give opportunity for direction of interests that might otherwise seek satisfaction in delinquent behavior, many girls and boys who could benefit from these programs are not attracted to them.

There is a paucity of programs for girls, even though the outstanding work of the Girl Scouts, Camp Fire Girls, YWCA and Big Sisters is known to all of us, and various sororities, women's clubs and many federally funded programs have projects for girls. Special attention should be given to girls in congested areas and minority groups; girls with physical, mental and emotional handicaps, and delinquent girls or girls with behavior problems who may need individual attention and guidance.

The authors recommend that greater emphasis be placed on providing community programs that will assist parents in fulfilling their responsibilities to their children and in helping to strengthen the family. Special attention should be given to girls, taking into consideration their constitutional, biological and psychological differences and their social position in our male-dominated culture. The female offender's goal, as any woman's, is a happy and successful marriage; therefore, her self-image is dependent upon the establishment of satisfactory relationships with the opposite sex.[2] The double standard for sexual behavior on the part of the male and the female must be recognized.

We cannot avoid the moral problems of the slums, of poverty and inequalities of justice. Those social problems which contribute to delinquent and criminal behavior must be attacked. Poor housing, slums, inadequate education, unemployment, under-employment, racism and injustices—all these must be eliminated.

In the histories of the delinquent girls, parental deprivation and abuse seemed to occur frequently. Hallack supports this finding and describes a common dynamic pattern as follows:

> The child receives inadequate nurturance and insufficient attention from her mother. As she reaches latency she begins to seek these same gratifications from her father. Particularly when the parents do not meet one another's needs, the father is likely to to develop an overly close relationship with the child. Erotic impulses intervene and the relationship between daughter and father takes on a latent sexual quality. With the onset of adolescence and sexual maturity this close relationship cannot be maintained without the danger of violating incestual taboos. At this point the father becomes more distant and the daughter turns to other men or boys and seeks their affection and love with desperate intensity. The price for affection is usually sexual intercourse. The potential delinquent then seeks gratification of basic oral needs through sexual activity, but since she rarely finds what she is looking for she moves through a variety of unsatisfying and frustrating sexual relationships. There are several revariations of this pattern. The erotic component of the relationship with the father often becomes threatening to the girl. She fears the incestual consequences of her own impulses and attempts to resolve the problem by leaving the disturbing situation. This encourages such behavior as running away. A surprisingly large percentage of delinquent girls claim that their first initiation to sexual experiences occurred during latency and that their seductor was an older man.[3] Misconceptions about the extent of homosexuality "honey-business" or "make believe" families in girls' institutions have led to serious false accusations and unfavorable newspaper publicity. It is important that not only personnel in an institutional setting, but the public as well have some understanding or awareness of the dynamics of group living. It is especially important that training school personnel understand the dynamics of female informal group structure—to understand the make-believe family which is pecularily suited to meet strongly ingrained dependency needs and the temporary aspirations of delinquent girls. To reduce its negative aspects as a repository for delinquent values and to motivate it toward positive goals requires reorientation from highly individualized procedures to the increased utilization of group methods and activities which can

sublimate narcissistic and exhibitionistic tendencies of girls and the use of techniques which will lessen the social gap between staff and girls. Such programs do not deny the existence of the make-believe family, but utilize it as a treatment force in changing delinquent values.[4]

Staff members in institutions should recognize that close friendships between adolescents are necessary and desirable. They should recognize that whenever children are isolated in a closed institution some sexual activity between members of the same sex will inevitably take place. Understanding this phenomenon is extremely important to the well-being of the girls as well as the morale of the staff members. They should recognize that there are very few true homosexuals and the so-called "honey-business" is an expression of normal needs to seek friendship and acceptance in whatever manner the girls can in an alien environment such as the training school, where they have been isolated from family, friends, acquaintances and familiar surroundings. They are emotionally deprived girls seeking attention. The vast majority of homosexual activities of girls are situational, since only a few are lesbians in the community. Most of the "butches" and their "lovers" are not true homosexuals—when they leave the institution they immediately return to normal relationships, some to promiscuous sexual activity as in the case of June W. who talked of the "honey business" at the training school, but engaged in many sexual activities with males in the community. It was also determined that she was seductive with the foster father whom she accused of "going with her and other girls." She later denied this allegation.

Halleck has so ably stated that there is always some danger that staff members in institutions will increase the problem of homosexual behavior by becoming obsessed with it. He concludes that the institution which takes a firm but casual attitude toward homosexuality and attends to the more urgent problems of establishing a treatment program will reap the rewards of stability and therapeutic success. Homosexual behavior is more prevalent in those training schools which do not have adequate treatment programs. An increase in such behavior in any institution usually indicates some breakdown in the program and greater distrust between the adolescents and the staff.

Helen Deutsch states that the development of youthful crushes for members of the same sex during latency and early adolescence is acceptable for the girl and is regarded as a property of normal female psychological development.[6]

The commitment of pregnant girls to state training schools has long been a controversial subject. Differential treatment according to class is clearly evident in the commitment of pregnant girls, oftentimes because of lack of other resources. It is generally true that our society is inclined to treat sexual deviation as a form of illness or immaturity if it occurs in the middle or upper-class people and as a crime if it occurs in lower-class people.[7] The double-standard exists even in the lower class—the girl is being sent away and the male usually remains free. The authors recommend that greater efforts be made to establish and to strengthen programs at the community level for working with unwed mothers. The experimental pilot project of the Florence Crittenden Association in Chicago under the directorship of Mrs. Mattie Wright is an example of constructive efforts in this regard.

Although a number of the case histories and girls' own stories indicated that after-care or parole planning involved foster home placement, most of the girls, as in the case of delinquent boys also, must return to the same environment which contributed to their delinquent behavior and subsequent commitment to the training school. Foster parents are reluctant to take delinquents. Problems encountered by the adolescent child in foster homes are familiar to many. The various aspects of these are too involved to be properly treated here. However, it should be stressed that there is need for good substitute homes for delinquent girls who can respond to this type of relationship. Residential group homes and halfway houses are needed especially. The few residential group homes for girls in existence in the Chicago area serve a limited and restricted group.

Alternatives to institutional treatment should be given primary consideration wherever indicated by judges, court officials and all involved in correctional work. Treatment should be individu-

alized. Institutionalization should be for those who require ex- ✓
ternal controls, who may be a danger to themselves or to society.
Group homes are needed for the girl who cannot respond to the
emotional demands of substitute or foster parents; for the girl who
has no home to return to and is too immature to adapt to independent living: and for the girl who does not require commitment
to an institution, but who is sufficiently stable and has the ability
to respond to community resources and treatment when her own
family and home have detrimental effects.

The Community Treatment Project of the California Department of Youth[8] is an example of an approach to treatment which
we recommend highly. It is based on two assumptions: (1) that not
all delinquents are alike, and (2) that delinquency can be sub-
divided into types which have clear cut implications for kinds of
treatment. They are as follows:

Delinquent Subtype	
Asocial Agressive, Asocial Passive	Needs a supportive environment to meet their unmet dependency needs. Foster home recommended.
Conformist, Immature Confirmist, Cultural Manipulator	Needs the involvement of an adult, a community agent who can express concern for the youth by controlling his behavior. Group treatment is used in order to change youth's attitudes by increasing his social perception.
Neurotic (Acting Out), Neurotic (Anxious Situational Emotional Reaction), Cultural Identifier	Needs to reduce the internal conflict of youth by increasing his insight into his personal and family dynamics. Family group therapy and group treatment are used.

Gisela Konopka has identified some concepts which are helpful
in understanding and treating the delinquent girl. They are the
unique, dramatic biological onset of puberty in the girl; the complex identification problem; the changing cultural position of
women; and the faceless adult authority and the resulting loneliness.[9]

In considering treatment models for the delinquent girl, as with other delinquent children, one is faced with the grim reality that our society should reevaluate its entire correctional justice system. Involuntary commitment to correctional institutions for children who are victims of circumstances through no fault of their own would lead only to hostility. resentment and a reinforcement of any negative tendencies toward society and the authorities in that society. With the recent court decisions and greater emphasis on the rights of children in juvenile court legislation, the future may prove brighter in this area.

In addition to treatment methods already mentioned in working with delinquents, behavior therapy is being utilized. Operant conditioning as a technique for changing behavior should be explored further in considering new approaches to therapy. A study of B. F. Skinner's works and other researches in this technique would serve to stimulate further research toward application in the correctional field. The Reception and Diagnostic Center for Boys and the Valley View School for Boys of the Illinois Department of Corrections, Juvenile Division are currently engaged in such a project. In the Tennessee State Institution for Girls, behavior-shaping techniques of educo-therapy have been used with remarkable success. The delinquent is often the under-achiever in school, and therefore learning disabilities are high in correctional institutions. If delinquent behavior is subsequent to the learning disability, a treatment model should focus on remediation of education deficits. To remedy the educational deficits and to change maladaptive behavior utilizing the disciplines of psychology and education in an intensive treatment program would bring about positive results in other correctional institutions just as was the experience in Tennessee.[11]

The disproportionate number of black girls committed to state training schools clearly points out several areas affecting these girls in our modern society. The conflicts and frustrations of the normal adolescent are compounded when applied to the delinquent girl, and more so for the delinquent black girl. Self-identity problems, negative feminine narcissism, loneliness, physical characteristics and environmental influences are all heightened in the case of black girls as contrasted with their white counterparts.

Grier and Cobbs[12] succinctly state that in this country the standard is the blond, blue-eyed, white-skinned girl with regular features. The black girl is, in fact, the antithesis of American beauty. However loved she may be by her mother, family and community, she has no real basis of feminine attractiveness on which to build a sound feminine narcissism. When to her physical unattractiveness is added a discouraging, depreciating mother-family-community environment, there is a damaged self-concept and an impairment of her feminine narcissism which will have profound consequences for her character development.[13]

However, in recent times the "black is beautiful" campaign, the new black-power movements, the development of pride and dignity in being black with African features and kinky hair is taking on historical significance. Through the influence of groups and individuals such as Dr. Kermit Mehlingher, a psychiatrist in Chicago, the advertising media is beginning to feature black persons.

This movement has contributed significantly not only to civil rights issues, but to individual self-pride and to instilling in the black person a feeling of pride, dignity and worth. It is hoped that there will be a more widespread identification of blacks with the community and neighborhood, with increased pride and respect for the value of property and of life. Perhaps the "black is beautiful" movement will help the black girl to increase her femininity and personal satisfaction as a black woman rather than causing her to struggle with the problems and conflicts of attempting to emulate her white counterpart.

In considering the delinquent girl, one must consider the whole field of law enforcement and corrections in the context of the entire area of juvenile and youthful offenders.

Certainly, the entire system requires reevaluation and is in dire need of innovative methods of treating young offenders. Community-based programs; group work methods and techniques; refinements in case work approaches; alternatives to institutionalization; educational, academic and vocational training, more relevant to needs and opportunities; better trained personnel, adequate funding and an enlightened public and press—all are important in this field.

Inconsistencies in the law concerning juveniles should be corrected. In many cases adults are given more consideration than children.

Children should not be punished for an offense which if committed by an adult would not be considered a violation of the law. In an adult court, a person who commits a crime but is found to be mentally incompetent is not considered responsible for his actions and is hospitalized if necessary. Delinquent boys and girls in Illinois who are found to be mentally incompetent are occasionally committed to the state correctional facility because of a lack of adequate community resources or insufficient facilities. The delinquent "tag" remains with them even after they have been committed to the state hospital or to the state school for the mentally retarded. The authors recommend that in no circumstances should a training school for delinquents be utilized as a holding agency for commitable mentally ill or mentally retarded children.

In the institutional commitment process it should be recognized that girls' dependency needs are much greater than boys' and that the process of adjudication is often more traumatic. The girl comes to the training school with an overwhelming need for acceptance often covered by a veneer of boredom, fear or hostility. She is prone to react with hostility and hysterical outburst.

Since her delinquency is highly individualized, more so than ever in our history, it is important to have an understanding of the dynamics of racial discrimination, prejudice and of black self-hatred. The hopeless child, who identified with her oppressor psychologically in an attempt to escape, turns on black people with aggression and hostility and hates them, besides herself.[14]

The vast majority of lower-class girls, especially black girls, are committed to training schools because of a lack of community resources or because their families were unable to care for them or rejected them. They are most often victims of impoverished circumstances. The upper-middle or upper-class girl is seldom committed to a training school. It should be no surprise to anyone that after a period of institutionalization the lower-class girl who is labeled delinquent does become hardened, resentful, angry and antisocial.

In the area of juvenile probation and parole, the authors recommend utilizing this rehabilitative resource more liberally. Much education is needed in this area, since most of the public and some professionals use these terms interchangeably.

In Chapter 7 the subject of probation was discussed in connection with the citing of cases of probation violations. Parole or aftercare is an extremely important part of the entire treatment and rehabilitation program of a child after leaving the training school. The community cannot expect the training school to completely change behavior in a child it has failed to do so for itself. The child must eventually return to society faced with reestablishing herself within the realities of her community. Skilled help is imperative during this transitional period and as well, all available resources should be mobilized to assist her. Yet, it is paradoxical to expect a community, which has previously failed, to mobilize resources which it lacks. Often, by the time the girl is ready to return, the community has deteriorated and the family is less ready to receive the child. In many cases, the best that can be expected is that the girl has gained some inner strengths to cope with a difficult and hopeless situation. It is not surprising that the recidivism rate of boys and girls in the correctional system is 50 per cent. Social action programs are vital in correcting this problem.

It is widely recognized that in general there is a great need for an adequate and efficient aftercare program. Politics should play no part in this vital and far-reaching program. Qualified personnel with proper supervision, in-service training and staff development programs are greatly needed in most states. The use of case aides or volunteers should be explored further in the aftercare program as well as in the institutional program. Although there is disagreement as to the type of training desirable for a parole officer or after-care worker, these are essentially casework jobs, and therefore training in a school of social work with field-work placement in the areas of corrections of delinquency is highly desirable. Some universities are offering advanced training in corrections and developing departments in this area. If the field of probation and parole is upgraded professionally, perhaps greater concentrated efforts would be made to raise salaries—both of these accomplishments would no doubt attract and retain competent personnel who are willing to work in an authoritative agency. There is indeed a challenge and a responsibility for professional personnel to come out of the "comfort of their ivory towers" where clients come to them, and to reach out and extend themselves to the hard-to-reach, the unmotivated and the so-called nonamenable ones. In the correctional field there is an acute need for more competent personnel. It appears that there is a great misconception among some social workers in particular, that the use of authority in casework is contrary to sound casework principles. More research is needed in the area of probation and parole as well as in the entire field of corrections.

In the final analysis, everyone must share part of the responsibility for the high incidence of juvenile delinquency and crime. Delinquency and crime cannot be effectively prevented or controlled without community interest and social action programs. Everyone should support agencies and programs designed to reduce or control delinquent behavior. The local community, especially in urban areas, is no longer firmly integrated by the interlocking primary groups of family and neighborhood. The latter once constituted the principal context of social control and of "living" in general for most people—particularly for children. But more and more, these primary groups compete with other groups.

Attitudes of the "modern" community still pose serious problems in relation to juvenile delinquency. The public attitude and understanding of crime and delinquency is about at the same level that medicine was at the beginning of the 19th century. The community's attitude toward youth offenders, like its treatment of youth generally, is a mixture of soft-heartedness, exasperation, wounded resignation and sadistic pleasure in punishment.

No type of human behavior is more important in time of stress and uncertainty than community leadership. Yet, public reaction to juvenile delinquency and criminality remains laden with emotional hysteria and misunderstanding. Apprehending and punishing seem more satisfying and appealing to the public than preventing, understanding and treating. This does not imply that offenders should be "coddled."

The injustices perpetrated against boys and girls under the guise of treatment should be recognized as a cause of increasing their rebelliousness and diminishing their sense of responsibility. Although the delinquent is given a civil commitment by a juvenile court, he is subjected to correctional procedures which include parole procedures that are similar to those procedures used with adult criminals. The authors question the fact that a runaway girl, a sex delinquent or a habitual truant should be subjected to the same paroling procedures as a felon or an adult who has committed a criminal offense such as murder.

The community should assume its responsibility and obligation to provide appropriate nonpunitive resources or institutions for those who are not guilty of crime and should be equipped to serve their needs. The various mixtures of a wide range of offenses and crimes, personalities and emotional problems in a single highly populated correctional institution are not conducive to providing an effective treatment program.

The self-defeating quality of the delinquent girl has been graphically illustrated. However, there is an increasing number of girls who engage in delinquent behavior which is also damaging to others. The authors note that female delinquency today appears to be more like male delinquency. Girls are becoming more involved in aggressive antisocial behavior, fighting, stealing and gang activities. Yet, it is understandable that as the social roles of boys and girls become more alike, their delinquent activities become less distinguishable from one another. The significant influence of the increasing emancipation of women and the proliferation of equal rights movements are both contributing factors in this change. Considering the direction our modern society is taking it will not be unreasonable to expect more serious female delinquency and crime in the future.[15]

However, the challenge is to mobilize all resources to combat the evils in our society—to redouble our efforts in instilling moral and spiritual values and in providing adequate housing, quality education and job opportunities for all.

So directing our efforts will produce the kind of society and the kind of community in which all girls and all children will be able to grow and to mature into worthwhile productive citizens able to develop their full potential.

REFERENCES

1. Long, Harvey L.: The church's mission and delinquents. *Federal Probation,* December, 1963, p. 30.
2. Payak, Bertha J.: Understanding the female offender. *Federal Probation,* December, 1963, p. 11.
3. Halleck, Seymour L.: *Psychiatry and the Dilemmas of Crime.* New York, Harper, 1967, pp. 141, 142.
4. *Institutional Rehabilitation of Delinquent Youth.* Albany, Delmar, p. 170.
5. Ibid., pp. 280, 281.
6. Deutch, Helene: *The Psychology of Women.* New York, Grune, 1944, Vol. 1, p. 85.
7. Ibid., p. 177.
8. The Community Treatment Project After Five Years, State of California, Department of Youth Authority.
9. Konopka, Gisela: *The Adolescent Girl in Conflict.* Englewood Cliffs, P-H, 1966, p. 119.
10. Study of Emotionally Disturbed Children. Interdepartmental Committee on Children and Youth of the Illinois Commission on Children, November, 1967, p. 81.
11. Rice, Ruth Dianne: Educo-therapy: A new approach to delinquent behavior. Reprinted from the Proceedings, 76th Annual Convention American Psychological Association, 1968. See Mary Harrington Hall.
12. Grier, William H., and Cobbs, Price M.: *Black Rage.* New York, Basic, 1968, p. 41.
13. Hall, Mary Harrinton: An interview with "Mr. Behaviorist," B. F. Skinner. *Psychology Today,* Sept. 1967, pp. 21-23, 68-70.
14. Grier and Price, op cit., p. 199.
15. Halleck, op. cit., p. 139.

SUGGESTED ADDITIONAL READINGS

Arnold, W. R.: Race and ethnicity relative to other factors in juvenile court dispositions. *Am J Sociol,* 77:211-227, September, 1971.
Barker, Gordon H., and Adams, William T.: Comparison of the delinquencies of boys and girls. *Journal of Criminal Law, Criminology and Police Science,* December, 1962, pp. 470-475.

Barzina, L.: *From Caesar to the Mafia.* New York, The Library Press, 1971.

Behrman, S. N.: People in a diary, I. *The New Yorker, 48*:13, 36-94, May, 1972.

Berkowitz, L., and Macaulay, J.: The contagion of criminal violence. *Sociometry, 34*:238-260, June, 1971.

Bryan, Helen: *Inside.* Boston, Houghton, 1953.

Cavan, Ruth Shonle (ed.): *Readings in Juvenile Delinquency,* 2nd ed. Philadelphia, Lippincott, 1969.

Chilton, R. J., and Markle, G. E.: Family disruption, delinquent conduct, and the effect of subclassification. *Am Sociol Rev, 37*:93-99, February, 1972.

Cressey, Donald R., and Ward, David A.: *Delinquency, Crime and Social Process.* New York, Harper, 1969.

Dana, Richard H.: The impact of fantasy on a treatment program. *Corrective Psychiatry,* pp. 202-212, July, 1964.

Erickson, M. L.: The group context of delinquent behavior. *Social Problems, 19*:114-129, Summer, 1971.

Fader, Daniel N., and Shaevitz, Morton H.: *Hooked on Books.* New York, Berkey, 1966.

Ferdinand, Theodore N.: *Typologies of Delinquency.* New York, Random, 1966.

Ferdinand, Theodore N.: The offense patterns and family structures of urban, village and rural delinquents. *Journal of Criminal Law, Criminology and Police Science,* pp. 86-93, March, 1964.

Feshbach, S., and Singer, R. D.: *Television and Aggression.* San Francisco, Jossey-Bass, 1971.

Friedman, Helen L.: The mother-daughter relationship; its potential in treatment of young unwed mothers. *Social Casework.* pp. 502-506, October, 1966.

Gastil, R. D.: Homicide and a regional culture of violence. *Am Sociol Rev, 36*:412-427, June, 1971.

Giallombardo, Rose: *Society of Women.* New York, Wiley, 1966.

Glasser, William: *Mental Health or Mental Illness.* New York, Harper, 1960.

Glen, Jeffrey E.: Developments in juvenile and family court law. *Crime and Delinquency,* pp. 295-305, April, 1969.

Glueck, S., and Glueck, E.: *Toward a Typology of Juvenile Offenders: Implications for Therapy and Prevention.* New York, Grune and Stratton, 1970.

Graham, F. P.: Black crime: The lawless image. *Harper's Magazine, 241*:64-78, September, 1970.

Gray, Madeline: *The Normal Woman.* New York, Scribner, 1967.

Hanson, Kitty: *Rebels in the Streets.* Englewood Cliffs, P-H, 1964.

Hersko, Marvin: Community therapy in an institution for delinquent girls. *Federal Probation,* pp. 41-46, June, 1964.

Jones, J.: *Prejudice and Racism.* Reading, Addison-Wesley, 1972.

Kilson, M.: An American Profile; The black student militant. *Encounter, 37:*83-90, September, 1971.

Kvaraceus, William C. *et al: Delinquent Behavior,* Volume I, *Culture and the Individual,* Volume II. *Principles and Practices.* Washington, Nat Educ Assoc, 1960.

Liebert, R. M., and Baron, R. A.: Some immediate effects of televised violence on children's behavior. *Developmental Psychology, 6:*469-475, May, 1972.

MacRae, Robert: Social work and social action. *The Social Service Review,* pp. 1-8, March, 1966.

Mathew, J. R.: Psychiatric semantics: "casing." *Corrective Psychiatry,* pp. 219-222, 4th quarter, 1963.

McCandless, B. R., *et al:* Perceived opportunity, delinquency, race and body build among delinquent youth. *Journal of Consulting and Clinical Psychology, 38:*281-287, April, 1972.

Menninger, Karl: *The Crime of Punishment.* New York, Viking, 1968.

Metzger, L. P.: American sociology and black assimilation; Conflicting perspectives. *Am J Sociol, 76:*627-647, January, 1971.

Nettler, Gwynn: A measure of alienation. *Am Sociol Rev, 22:*670-677, December, 1957.

_____: Antisocial sentiment and criminality. *Am Sociol Rev, 24:*202-218, April, 1959.

_____: Review, The subculture of violence. *Social Forces, 46:*427-428, March, 1968.

_____: *Explanations.* New York, McGraw, 1970.

_____: Shifting the Load. *Am Behav Sci, 15:*361-379, January-February, 1972.

_____: Knowing and doing. *The American Sociologist, 7:*3-7, February, 1972.

Power, M. J. *et al:* Neighborhood, school and juveniles before the courts. *The British Journal of Criminology, 12:*111-132, April, 1972.

Quinney, Richard: *Crime and Justice in Society.* Boston, Little, 1969.

Rowles, Burton J.: *The Lady at Box 99.* New York, Seabury, 1962.

Rubin, Sol: Developments in correctional law. *Crime and Delinquency,* pp. 283-294, April, 1969.

Salem, R. G., and Bowers, W. J.: Severity of formal sanctions as a deterrent to deviant behavior. *Law and Society Review, 5:*21-40, August, 1970.

Scherz, Frances H.: The crisis of adolescence in family life. *Social Casework,* pp. 209-215, April, 1967.

Schuessler, Karl, and Slatin, Gerald: The MMPI characteristics of incarcerated females. *Crime and Delinquency*, pp. 119-126, July, 1964.

Stein, A. H. *et al*: Television content and young children's behavior. In Murray, J. P. *et al* (eds): *Television and social behavior*, Vol. 2. *Television and social learning*. Washington, U.S. Government Printing Office, 1971.

Task Force Report: Juvenile Delinquency and Youth Crime. The President's Commission on Law Enforcement and Administration of Justice, U.S. Government Printing Office, Washington, 1967.

Task Force Report: Corrections. The President's Commission on Law Enforcement and Administration of Justice, U.S. Government Printing Office, Washington, 1967.

Thomas, W. I.: *The Unadjusted Girl*. Boston, Little, 1923.

Thomas, A., *et al*: The origin of personality. *Scientific American, 223*: 102-109, August, 1970.

Torjo, Romalo: An exploratory study of cottage reputation in a training school for girls. *Crime and Delinquency*, pp. 110-118, July, 1964.

Trese, Leo John: *101 Delinquent Girls*. Notre Dame, Fides, 1962.

Unkovic, Charles M., and Duscay, William O.: Objectives of training schools for delinquents. *Federal Probation*, pp. 49-52, March, 1969.

Waldo, G. P., and Chiricos, T. G.: Perceived penal sanction and self-reported criminality. A neglected approach to deterrence research. *Social Problems, 19*:522-540, Spring, 1972.

Ward, R. H.: The laveling theory: A critical analysis. *Criminology, 9*:268-290, August-November, 1971.

Weisman, Irving: Offender status; role behavior and treatment considerations. *Social Casework*, pp. 422-425, July, 1967.

Willing, M. K.: *Beyond Conception: Our Children's Children*. Boston, Gambit, 1971.

AUTHOR INDEX

A

Abrahamsen, D., 24, 32
Adams, W. T., 162
Aichorn, A., 22, 23, 32, 39
Ames, R., 66
Annual Report, Department of Youth
  Authority, Health and Welfare
  Agency, State of California, 6, 13
Arnold, W. R., 162
Augustus, J., 112
Axelrad, S., 130, 144

B

Ball, J. C., 85, 110
Barker, G. H., 162
Barnes, N. E., 37, 53
Baron, R. A., 164
Barzina, L., 163
Bates, J. E., 24, 32
Behrman, S. N., 163
Bell, M., 112, 128
Berkowitz, L., 163
Bernard, W., 29, 33
Bloch, H. A., 19, 26, 32, 52, 129, 144
Bowers, W. J., 164
Breed, A. F., 11
Brooks, D., 146
Bryan, H., 163
Butler, E. W., 47, 48, 52

C

Carr, L. J., 23, 26, 113
Cavan, R. S., 20, 32, 113, 128, 131, 144,
  163
Cayton, H. R., 42, 51
Chilton, R. J., 163
Chiricos, T. G., 165
Chute, C. L., 112, 128
Cobbs, P. M., 157, 162
Cohen, A. K., 26, 33, 37, 51
Collidge, J. C., 40, 51
Cooper, R., 84

Coughlin, R., 41, 51
Coulter, C. W., 19, 32
Cousineau, D. F., 33
Cressey, D. R., 163
Crystal, D., 112, 128

D

Dana, R. H., 163
Davis, A., 42, 51
Deutch, H., 154, 162
"Diverting Youth from the Correc-
  tional System", U.S. Dept. of
  Health, Education and Welfare, 13
Drake, St.C., 42, 51
Dressler, D., 86, 110
DuPre Lumpkin, K., 88
Duscay, W. O., 165

E

Ehrmann, W. W., 85, 110
Eissler, K. R., 51
Eleanor, T., 50
Ellington, J. R., 131, 144
Elliott, M. A., 68, 84, 87, 88, 110
England, R. W., Jr., 114, 128
Erickson, M. L., 163
Exner, 21

F

Fader, D. N., 163
Ferdinand, T. N., 163
Fernald, M. R., 35, 50
Ferrero, W., 50
Feshbach, S., 163
First Annual Report, Department of
  Corrections, State of Illinois, 13
Flynn, F. T., 19, 32, 52, 129, 144
Freud, S., 23
Friedlander, K., 22, 32
Friedman, H. L., 163
Fritz, D., 32

SUBJECT INDEX

B

Behavior therapy, 156
"Big five" offenses, 4-5, 145
  change in, 6
  incorrigibility and truancy, 9

C

Commitment, instituional, 3
  "big five" reasons leading to, 4-5, 145
    change in, 6
    incorrigibility and truancy, 9
  black girls, 4, 145
    "black is beautiful" movement, 157
  conflicts and frustrations, 156-157
  boys' and girls' delinquency court cases, 9-10
  California Youth Authority female juvenile first commitment, 8, 17-18
  California Youth Authority male/ female components, 6-7
  California Youth Authority male juvenile first commitment, 7
  charges leading to, 4-5
  in Illinois, 4, 6
  decline in, 11
  dependency needs of girls, 158
  diversion programs, 10-11
    decline in commitment, 11
    Illinois Unified Code of Corrections, 12-13
    Social Service Unit of the Wheaton Police Department, 12
  girls' court cases, increase in, 9-10
  Illinois Unified Code of Corrections, 12
  orders of disposition, 12-13
  lack of community resources, 158
  length of stay, 3
    factors affecting, 3-4
  lower-class girls, 158-159

Mexican, Indian or Puerto Rican girls, 4
  police arrest data, 9
  questionnaire to state institutions, 3-5
  states' costs for maintenance, 4, 145
  upper-middle or upper-class girls, 158
Community Treatment Project of the California Department of Youth, 155
  delinquent subtypes, 155
Cottage parents, 147-148

D

Delinquent girl, alternatives to institutional treatment, 154-155
  "bad girl" role, 86
  California Youth Authority female juvenile first commitment, 8, 17-18
  community services for, 145, 146, 147
  Community Treatment Project of the California Department of Youth, 155
  concepts for understanding and treating, 155
  coordination of services in institutions, 147
  cottage parents, selection and training of, 147-148
  court cases, increase in, 9-10
  dependency needs, 158
  diversified institutional programs, importance of, 147
  emancipation of women, 161
    (*see also* Female delinquency and and crime)
  family status, dependence on, 86
  foster home placement, 154
  incorrigible girl, 67-84
    (*see also* Incorrigible girl)

169